INSTANT KARMA & GRACE

The Mantra of a Calm Man

DOUG MCPHILLIPS

Also by Doug McPhillips

Novels:

From Darkness to Light

The Sword of Discernment.

Santiago Traveller.
We is Me Upside Down.
The Guru of Jerusalem.
Masters at My Table.
The Wicklow Way.
Ace McDice, Stretch Deed
& Moonshine Melody.

Guide book:

A Camino Guide Book.

Albums:

Country Camino.

Santiago Traveller.

Doug McPhillips 2022.

This book is copyright. Apart from fair dealing for the purpose of private study, research, criticism or review, as permitted under the Copyright Act, no part may be reproduced by any process whatsoever without the editor's written permission.

ISBN 978-0-6454221-2-2

National library of Australia catalogue in publication: Holy Bible, New International Version 1980 edition..Alcoholics..Anonymous..World..Series..2001.,Karma-in-Hinduism-Wikipedia. Psychology–today-Google.research-Authors.unknown.
Karma-University-Bristol.Philosophy Encyclopaedia-Britannica.
Assassinate!-Steven-Parissien,Quercus Publishing London 2008. The Qur'an- Abul Qasim Publishing House, 1997. National Council on Alcoholism and Drug Dependence (NCADD) • National Institute on Alcohol Abuse and Alcoholism (NIAAA) • National Institute on Drug Abuse

This book is a work of fiction. All characters in this novel are of the author's own making for the sake of the message herein. Any resemblance to actual events or locales or persons living or dead is entirely coincidental. Where poetic licence is used to turn fact into fiction, names have been changed to protect the innocent.

To those to whom I have offended,
I beg for forgiveness.
For those who have offended me,
I do forgive.

INTRODUCTION.

This little story is an account of one man applying to living the principles of karma according to his own interpretation. It comes from living experiences of decades of good, bad and indifferent attitude to circumstance that surrounded his life, the lesson learnt in the getting of wisdom in the matter of living life according to certain principles as a consequence. Firstly though, it must be said what is meant by 'karma,' in order for the writer to tell the tale that follows. Karma, or Ka:me, is not a verb, it's a noun. That is, it is not a saying, it's the name of a spiritual 'thing.' Hindu and Buddhist religions, based on the philosophy of Buddha define it as " the sum of a persons" actions in this and previous states of existence, viewed as deciding their fate in future existences.' This might simply be stated in a western psychological sense as good or bad luck, viewed as a result of one's actions.

The word karma means the result of a person's actions as well as the actions themselves. It is a terminology of the cycle of cause and effect. According to the theory of Karma, what happens to a person, happens because they caused it with their actions. In a logical sense it is real and present in our lives, an energy force of your will that can be controlled or tapped into for better or for worse. Lets face it, karma is very real and present in our lives, a kind of mystical, magical energy that we can't always understand through our linear, logical half brain notion of who we really are and what life is all about. You may take this viewpoint but depending upon your own experience have an entirely different idea of how karma applies or doesn't apply in your life. It is entirely up to you to consider the 'for and against the laws of karma,' as applied in this story and how they may work to better your living experience of significant misfortune in your life.

I trust that you the reader will benefit from this little story, for I will write it in consideration of your will for betterment of in offering forgiveness to those living and dead who have offended and that whom whom have offended. I seek further insight into the forces that surround us collectively and as spiritual beings. For it may well be only in by writing this it may bring as a consequence of my reactions to the karma that surrounds me that I have become more spiritually sound to my journey of acceptance of the life as it is now. It is as it is my intention here to examine my consciousness of the journey taken thus far as it is to reflect on the majestic mystery presence of the 'thing called karma,' to bring new wisdom to my purpose and understanding of living life whatever befalls me in the present and the future.

Karma it seems is a cyclical thing and carries various intensity on its ensuing return. The action or reaction according to the turn of events at the time is a new getting of wisdom or a failure to take on board the learned experience for one's new or renewed betterment. The acceptance or fight back against the forces of karma in current living is an ultimate lesson in our eventual fate.

It seems that God created the laws of karma for us to learn to use the forces of given courage and strength provided by him or to mistakenly become dependent upon our fateful ego and defective character to enter into despair and calamity before we collapse into his care. It is then that one's state of mind can turn into a miracle of recovery, a miracle of mindful creative energy guided by him, and or the muses that influence the imagination of the individual. Ultimately the fate eternal of the pilgrim on this path of a new reality and zest for living embraces God given belief in the present moment of logical wisdom and imaginary creative understanding. Thus, living the karma that arises, good, bad or indifferent, to accept as a lesson from the God of one's own understanding, not so much to embrace it by taking it on board, but to encounter and chance to live the fate it inflicts upon one's heart and soulfulness. For once we accept the karma then and only then will the lesson be learnt to move on to yet another karma in the moment.

If one accepts the mythology of Karma, it seems it is stored in the individual's soul in three varieties. That which one has chosen in the process of our particular present birth, that which is stored for later births; (resurrection if you will to a new life after death); and the new karma you generate the moment you live in the present to utilise more efficiently in the now and future existence. Just as many believe in a new resurrection after death, equally many believe in a prior lifetime of long standing influence on our souls in the current life. So apart from the karma that has us in the present of negative or positive consequence, we have those of past lives to deal with too. So if we are to erase past bad karma experiences that we did not face in the course of past lifetimes or indeed in the course of our present one, we at some stage come back to face and finish them. In addition to the different varieties of karma, there are also 12 laws or rules to live by for our betterment. These laws originated from the Hindu and Buddhist belief systems. They relate to cause and effect, creation, humility, growth, responsibility, connection, focus, giving and receiving, the present, change, patience and reward. Suffice to say we shall embrace these laws during the course of this story. But for now let us venture into the events of the life that led the teller of this tale to 'Instant Karma.'

Content:

Introduction: 5.

Chapter 1. A Fall from Grace. 9.

Chapter 2. The workings of Reincarnation. 19.

Chapter 3. Karmic falls to Grace. 29.

Chapter 4. Avatars of Goodwill & Grace. 37.

Chapter 5. Legends on foot. 51.

Chapter 6. Yoga and Meditation. 61.

Chapter 7. The healing power of AA. 69.

Chapter 8. A God of Logic and the Manifest. 77.

Chapter 9. Personal Stories. 91.

Chapter 10. Epilogue. 99.

Instant karma's gonna get you
Gonna knock you right on the head
You better get yourself together
Pretty soon you're gonna be dead

What in the world you thinking' of
Laughing in the face of love
What on earth you trying to do
It's up to you, yeah you

Instant karma's gonna get you
Gonna look you right in the face
Better get yourself together darling'
Join the human race

How in the world you gonna see
Laughing at fools like me?
Who on earth d'you think you are
A super star? Well right, you are

Well, we all shine on
Like the moon and the stars and the sun
Well, we all shine on
Everyone come on

Instant karma's gonna get you
Gonna knock you off your feet
Better recognise your brothers
Everyone you meet

Why in the world are we here?
Surely not to live in pain and fear
Why on…

    Instant Karma- John Lennon.

CHAPTER 1

A FALL FROM GRACE

Many Christians believe him to be once a beautiful angel named Lucifer, the morning star, the first light of day before the fall. He dishonoured his angelic post in manipulating the natural order God had established in an attempt to raise himself higher than God in a complete reversal of his entire being and status. According to God, one cannot become more than they already are. Lucifer was another spirit son of God, who rebelled against the plan's reliance on the ability and privilege God gives us to choose and act for ourselves. For God's agency is
essential in the plan of salvation, without this plan's reliance we would not be able to learn or progress or to follow our Saviour. Lucifer, or Satan if you will, as punishment for his disobedience and the grave dishonouring of his angelic post was cast out of heaven with an army of angels who followed him. "How you have fallen from heaven, O Lucifer, son of the morning! how art thou cut to the ground which didst weaken the nations!" Isaiah 14:12. and in Luke 10: "The Morning Star fell like lightning from the heavens."

There were apparently many angels other than Lucifer who were cast out of heaven at the fall. The name of these devil entities from both Christian and Pagan mythology, such as Moloch, Chemosh, Belial, Beelzebub joined Lucifer, who convinced many angel followers to live free from the laws of God thereupon they too were cast out of heaven into eternal darkness. So these angels, under the guidance of Lucifer the Satan accuser, who also fulfils the role of the Angel of Death, denied the existence of truth in the order of good in the heavens and on earth, cast a spiritual wound in the soul of mankind in offending Godly purpose. According to Abrahamic religions, "fallen angels" appears neither in the Bible nor other Abrahamic scriptures, but is used to describe angels cast from heaven who wronged God. Such angels often tempt humans into doing wrong through the defects of their character inherited since the time of the fall.

In a powerful example of the myths and legends of the fall of man in accord with the guidance of Lucifer, is the historical and biblical story of Nebuchadnezzar 11, powerful ruler and the longest reigning king of Babylon who reigned from BC, August 605-until his death 7th October 562. This Emperor King defied God's natural agency manipulating the order of his Empire. Nebuchadnezzar strengthened Babylon and brought it into its golden years, in which after his demise his offspring quickly tarnished and ended up destroying the nation. As a warrior king, he wasted no time and began his conquest of the nations of his era, similar to Alexander the Great centuries later. The decline of the Assyrian Empire between 600 BC and later 500 BC, left a gap wide open for the next global superpower to take over.

He began to take over surrounding nations, chiefly among those was Israel. For a while Israel kept Babylon's influence apart from their own by paying a certain price for their "protection." But in reality the wealth they distributed to Babylon ensured the superpower wouldn't sack and pillage their nation as it continued to do with others in the expansion of the Babylonian Empire. Eventually Jehoiakim, the King of Israel then known as Judah, refuses to pay any further tribute to Babylon. An enraged Nebuchadnezzar lays siege to Israel, starving and pillaging the nation. He proceeded to take the Israelites' captives in three waves, then put a puppet king in charge. This king rebels and Nebuchadnezzar nearly destroys Israel, leaving a remnant of the poorest of the poor behind.

The might of King Nebuchadnezzar's reign seems like he was channelling a direct link to the might and power of the evil karma of Lucifer at the time of his attempt to change the natural order of God's plan. This King of the earthly realm conquered Syria and Palestine and made Babylon a splendid city, destroyed the temple of Jerusalem and initiated the captivity of the Jewish population. But like all who defy the will of God and block their own inner good karma, he was a classic arrogant fellow who believed that he was the centre of the universe. Like Lucifer, he displayed a plethora of defects of character that ultimately brought him undone. In the biblical prophecy of Daniel, chapter 4, he speaks of God stripping Nebuchadnezzar of his crown and of him losing his sanity. ["He was driven away from people and for seven years lived like an animal and ate grass like an ox. His body was drench with the dew of heaven until his hair grew like the feathers of an eagle and his nails like the claws of a bird."] In Isaiah 16-17 we read [" Is this the man who shook the earth and made the kingdoms tremble, who turned the world into a desert and destroyed its cities,…]

Although he had pillaged, killed and deposed kings he was ultimately forgiven by God after he suffered much in his insanity of embracing bad karma over good karma. So it came to pass that Nebuchadnezzar regained his sanity, overcame his defects of character and returned to God's good karma. Whilst the king achieved great wealth for his nation and prosperity for his people, he was humbled by God for boasting about his achievements. He learnt his lesson: "Now I, Nebuchadnezzar, praise and exalt and glorify the King of Heaven, because everything he does is right, and all his ways are just. And those who walk in pride he is able to be humbled." (Daniel 5:37)

Whilst the majority of the heavenly spirits of creation remained with God's natural order and plan for the universe, it shall be related herein as a process of understanding of their role in the order of Godly grace and karma shortly. But first, let us not forget that there were others who were influenced by Lucifer to reject the good grace of the plan of God's kingdom by delving into their own bad Karma of consciousness in preference to the will of their creator. The first of these in the order of the beginning of the earthly universe is mentioned in rabbinic literature as Lilith, who is variously depicted as the mother of Adam's demonic offspring following his separation from Eve as his first wife. Whereas Eve was created from Adam's rib (Genesis 2:22), some accounts hold that Lilith was the woman implied in Genesis 1:27 and was made from the same soil as Adam. She is depicted as the female figure in Mesopotamian and Judaic mythology, alternatively the first wife of Adam and supposedly the primordial she-demon. So Lilith is cited as having been "banished" from the garden of Eden for not complying with or obeying Adam, finally refusing to lay with him.

The Bible mentions Lilith only once, as a dweller in waste places (Isaiah 23:14), but she is depicted as a seducer or slayer of children which has a long history in Babylonian religion. She was sexually attracted to Lucifer as his first human earthly wife and was found in a cave bearing children by three angels. She refuses to return to God's grace and in revenge is said to rob children of life and is responsible for the deaths of still-born infants and crib deaths. In Isaiah 34:14 in various Bible translations interpreters often envision the figure of Lilith as a dangerous demon of the night who is sexually wanton, and who steals babies in the darkness. Lilith later wedded Eblis, the 'Prince of the devils,' and became the mother of demons and spectres and in vengeance upon her rival, even the mother of mankind, became the special enemy of babies. As for Lucifer's offspring, his daughter, known as the Angel Liberty, was created by God from a father left behind from a wing of Lucifer following his banishment from heaven. All this myth and story telling of the beginnings of the Universe speak of a fall but it equally tells of the outcome of bad karma over good karma and more to the point the rejection of supernatural grace given to humanity by God for our betterment.

As to the good karma at the beginning of time, and those of the heavenly host who stayed to administer and follow their maker, the prophet Isaiah tells us that there existed in the heavens a seraphim of six-winged " fiery" angels who surrounded God as he sits upon his exalted throne and who worship God continually (Isaiah 6). The seraphim also minister to the Lord and serve as His agents of purification, as demonstrated by their clearing of Isaiah's sins before he began his prophetic ministry. The word 'seraphim' means in Hebrew "to burn." The implication here is that these attendant angels burn in love of God. The seraphim seem to bear a resemblance to humans, as Isaiah described them as having faces, feet, hands and voices.(Isaiah 6:2-7). In Isaiah's vision the seraphim repeatedly proclaimed God's supreme holiness and glory. They in three fold repetition connoted God's wholeness as the beginning, the middle and the end. That of God's eternal nature which is the same yesterday, today and tomorrow; God's divine protection as seen in the Holy Trinity of Father, Son and Holy Spirit and God's complete Supreme holiness, unmatched by anything or anyone else. Where Isiah noticed the heavenly seraphim covered themselves before God to acknowledge their presence.

In the kingdom of heaven there exists Nine levels of spiritual beings which are grouped into three orders. The Seraphim Thrones of which we already spoke, then comes the middle order of Dominions Virtues Powers: Think of dominions as middle management. They receive orders from seraphim and cherubim, then dish out duties to the "worker bee" angels of the lower orders. Their main purpose is to make sure that the cosmos remains in order by sending down power to heads of government and other authority figures. Shaped like sparks of light, virtues are in charge of maintaining the natural world, and they inspire living things in areas such as science. They also take orders from the angels above and convert them into miracles for the deserving. When they make themselves known to us in their earthly form, they are musicians, artists, healers, and scientists who work with the power of love, as well as physics. The two angels at the ascension of Jesus are believed to have been virtues. Then come the Nine ranks of lower order of Holy leaders known as Archangels and according to sacred scripture these are mentioned; Michael, Gabriel Raphael, and Uriel as the prime adapters of God's word for humanity. Michael the Archangel, in the Bible and in the Qur'ān (as Mīkāl), is repeatedly depicted as the "great captain," the leader of the heavenly hosts, and the warrior helping the children of Israel. It was Michael as the faithful servitor of God who was given the task to hurl down from Heaven the arrogant and proud 'morning star' Lucifer together with the other fallen angels.

Gabriel comes next as the herald of visions, messenger of God and one of the angels of higher rank. He, in this life, makes God's message understandable to people and helps them to accept it with pure heart. So to adapt to good karma and holy grace, we the people get the message to help us on our spiritual journey towards the heavenly host in the present and hereafter. It has been written that Lucifer is one of the brothers of angelic trio-Gabriel, Michael and Lucifer who all lived in harmony until the seed of evil began to take root in him. Archangel Raphaels is said to guard pilgrims on their journeys and is often depicted holding a staff. Sometimes he is depicted as standing on a fish, which alludes to his healing of Tobit with the fish's gill in the bible. Early mosaics often show archangels dressed in the clothing of Byzantine couriers. So the interpretation of their duties in the spirit world may seem to appear as relating to Kings ands court officials. Other depictions have them shaped like ays of light who oversee everything. They guide our entire world nations, cities, and towns. What's more, they are in charge of religion and politics. As if their plate isn't full enough, they are also in charge of managing the earthly duties of the angels below them. But don't call on them to help you personally; archangels p respond best when dealing with matters involving all humankind. They are the first order of angels that appear only in human form. As such, they function among us as pioneers fro change ing the form of explorers, philosophers, and human rights leaders.

This order is most commonly known because they are mentioned by name in the Bible-Michael, Gabriel and Raphael. Then comes Uriel.

Archangel Uriel is known as the angel of wisdom. He shines the light of Gods' truth into the darkness of confusion. Uriel means "God is my light" or "fire of God." The faithful turn to Uriel for help seeking God's will before making decisions, learning new information, solving problems and resolving conflicts. They also turn to him for help letting go of destructive emotions such as anxiety and anger, which can prevent believers from discerning wisdom or recognising dangerous situations. In art, Uriel is often depicted carrying either a book or a scroll, both of which represent wisdom. Another symbol connected with Uriel is an open hand holding a flame or the sun, which represents God's truth. Like his fellow archangels, Uriel has an angelic energy colour, like the light in a rainbow, but in this case, red, which represents him and the work he performs. Some sources also attribute the colour yellow or gold to Uriel. This Archangel isn't mentioned in canonical religious texts from the world's major religions, but he is mentioned significantly in major religious apocryphal texts. Apocryphal texts are religious works that were included in some early versions of the Bible but today are considered to be secondary in importance to the scripture of the Old and New Testaments.

The Book of Enoch (part of the Jewish and Christian Apocrypha) describes Uriel as one of seven archangels who preside over the world. Uriel warns the prophet Noah about the upcoming flood in Enoch chapter 10. In Enoch chapters 19 and 21, Uriel reveals that the fallen angels who rebelled against God will be judged and shows Enoch a vision of where they are "bound until the infinite number of the days of their crimes be completed." (Enoch 21:3)

In the Jewish and Christian apocryphal text 2 Esdras, God sends Uriel to answer a series of questions that the prophet Ezra asks God. When answering Ezra's questions, Uriel tells him that God has permitted him to describe signs about good and evil at work in the world, but it will still be difficult for Ezra to understand from his limited human perspective. In 2 Esdras 4:10-11, Uriel asks Ezra: "You cannot understand the things with which you have grown up; how then can your mind comprehend the way of the Most High? And how can one who is already worn out by the corrupt world understand incorruption?" When Ezra asks questions about his personal life, such as how long he'll live, Uriel replies: "Concerning the signs about which you ask me, I can tell you in part; but I was not sent to tell you concerning your life, for I do not know." (2 Esdras 4:52) In various Christian apocryphal gospels, Uriel rescues John the Baptist from being murdered by King Herod's order to massacre young boys around the time of Jesus's birth. Uriel carries both John and his mother Elizabeth to join Jesus and his parents in Egypt.

The Apocalypse of Peter describes Uriel as the angel of repentance. In Jewish tradition, Uriel is the one who checks the doors of homes throughout Egypt for lamb's blood (representing faithfulness to God) during Passover, when a deadly plague strikes first-born children as a judgement for sin but spares the children of faithful families. At the next level below the nine of Archangels are those that might just be called "regular angels." They are guardians of people and all things physical and are the most common type of angels. These angels are sent as messengers to humanity. Personal guardian angels come from this category. Angels may also protect and warn humans as well as act as warriors on behalf of God.

I write of these things to give you the reader some insight (if you don't already know) into the order of things in the universe at the time of God's creation, at the time of Lucifer's fall and the angels of disgrace and bad karma that has inflicted this world of ours from the beginning of time until the present day. It is as an aftermath of the beginning in accord with biblical and other religious tradition on which I reflect, as much as I do of myth and the majesty of the use of the imagination and not just the linear logical brain, be you believer or non believe; much can be learnt and adapted to one's own particular concept of what constitutes a higher power of influence in your life. I make no apology for leaning towards the creative forces of my belief in a higher power but it is up to you to decide if you accept or reject my belief. For my logical half brain can equally prove by adaptation of scientific 'so called proof' that there is no higher being, no God, no karma or grace.; just one big bang or evolutionary process that causes it all. But I hasten to add that like you I have a creative brain that lies in the image and likeness of a God creator and it houses an imagination and belief of a Godly force in my life. I have much to provide and prove by my own personal living experience that a God of my own understanding influences my life, exists as a guiding light, as do angelic forces, and that the scaffolding of my Christian upbringing provides a further light of understanding of my belief by symbols and signs, and, if you will, karma.

Let us not forget the fact that billions of people in the world follow religious systems that teach the law of karma; Buddhism, Hinduism and Sikhism of the east practice it and many Christians reflect a popularised concept of karma in their thinking. So, in incorporating the doctrine of karma with that of the biblical concept of grace I hope to give some further insight as to how I arrive at where I am with warm belief and that of grace; a supernatural gift beloved by Christians, imposed on us by God for our salvation, is far more relevant and powerful than the doctrine of karma, be that good or bad. Karma in its basic concept is the belief that our actions bring corresponding reactions. It may be expressed as getting what we deserve. Some see karma as a natural universal law, whereas others allow for a deity to control or dispense the effects of karma. The consequences of one's karma may be experienced in this life or in the future life, as in reincarnation, the belief that we shall return to live again in another form. I shall cover more on reincarnation later in another chapter.

The word karma means action or performance. In its most basic concept, karma is the belief that our actions bring corresponding reactions. In more popular terms, we get what we deserve or "what goes around comes around." Some see karma as a natural universal law, whereas others allow for a deity to control or dispense the effects of karma. The consequences of one's karma may be experienced in this life or in a future life (as in reincarnation, the belief that we return to live again in another form). In similarity with biblical truth there are some similarities between karma and truths we find in the Bible. What God has taught in the Bible is just, both in the sense that He punishes evil and rewards good. The book of Proverbs gives many principles that show good or bad actions bring good or bad consequences. Some point to Galatians 6:7: "Do not be deceived, God is not mocked; for whatever a man sows, that he will also reap."

Furthermore, the Bible teaches that these consequences for our actions can be experienced in this life or in the next. In this life, bad actions can have negative consequences like hindering our fellowship with God and people, poverty, physical illness, death, etc. Equally, good behaviour has contrasting good consequences. Though the Bible does not teach reincarnation, it does teach that believers have a future life in the kingdom of God. Good or bad actions in this life can diminish or enhance that experience in the kingdom (Matt.25:14-30; 2 Tim. 2:12; Rev. 22:12). The Bible does not teach that the universe is locked into karma or any universal law. Yes, God did design the universe to operate by some basic principles of justice and retribution, many of which are mentioned throughout the Bible. But God can alter the laws He has created and is not a slave to those principles. Though He is just, He is also loving, and His love for us can supersede His justice toward us. When it comes to our salvation, "He made Him [Jesus] who knew no sin, to free us from sin so that we might become the righteousness of God in Him" (2 Cor. 5:21). God fulfilled His justice by exacting payment for our sins, but He did it through His Son dying in our place. That is contrary to what karma expects. Because God loves us, and because His innocent Son satisfied His justice, God can give us His eternal life, His righteousness, and His forgiveness for all of our sins. By His grace through faith in His Son we are given what we do not deserve. While karma locks a person into a cycle of retributive justice, God breaks that cycle with His grace. Incidentally, the biblical use of the word 'sin' denotes many things that may be easily misunderstood. I prefer to call sin 'conscious error on my part as a consequence of my defects of character.'

While karma guarantees that a person gets what he deserves, grace guarantees that a person can get what he does not deserve. By definition grace is a free gift that is not deserved. The Bible teaches that God's grace can break into the cycle of sin with blessing. Consider Psalm 103:10 says [He has not dealt with us according to our sins, Nor punished us according to our iniquities.] And Rom. 5:8 says, [But God demonstrates His own love toward us, in that while we were still sinners, Christ died for us. Conversely, God also allows bad things to happen to very good people.]

In the Old Testament Job, is called the most righteous man on earth, yet he suffered horribly. In the New Testament God's perfect Son was unfairly condemned and crucified. But it must not be forgotten that Jesus allowed his own suffering and death on that cross to be as a perfect sacrifice in lieu of sacrificing a lamb offering to God, as Jewish religious tradition dictated. Jesus sacrificed himself so that mankind's sin may be forgiven.

The consequence of His being the 'Sacrificial Lamb' of God on our behalf without God's intervention to stop it, is believed by Christians to be the means by which humanity can tap into the Godhead through the Holy Spirit, the third person of the Trinity of Father, Son and Spirit. The way, if you will, for mankind to receive forgiveness for conscious wrongdoing from the heavenly Father, through the action of his sacrificial Son. The forgiveness of sin purified by God with heavenly grace administered through the Holy Spirit to within the tabernacle within every human soul.

God has free course to act outside of His normal design. This upends the rigid dictates of karma. Unlike reincarnation, which teaches that a person gets another life to improve his or her karma, the Bible does not teach that anyone gets a "do over" after this life. This removes any excuse to live irresponsibly now and postpone doing good things to another life. Christians believe all people will be held accountable to a judgement that comes after they die (Heb. 9:27) or when the Lord Jesus comes (John 5:28-29). For those who have not believed in Jesus Christ this is a judgement of their unbelief and evil deeds that earns them eternal damnation in the lake of fire (Rev. 20:13-15). For those who have believed in Jesus Christ this is an evaluation of their works at the Judgement Seat of Christ to see whether they are worthy of eternal rewards (Rom. 14:10-1; 2 Cor. 5:10). A closer look at Galatians 6:7.This passage clearly teaches that we reap what we sow, but several things should be noted. First, though it is stated as a divine principle, God has the freedom to override His own principles of retribution and reward. If He did not, no sinner could be saved. Also, to be faithful to the context of Galatians 6, this verse is not discussing the condition for eternal salvation, but the consequences for Christians who live either according to the Spirit or the flesh (Gal. 5:21-26). The emphasis in the context is admonishment for Christians to do good works as they live under grace instead of law. If Christians live by the Spirit (not the flesh), they will have a richer experience of God's eternal life in the future (6:8-9). This is not karma, but divine motivation and reward for personal responsibility.

Grace trumps karma. In karma there is no hope apart from what we can do for ourselves by our own effort. The Bible teaches and experience shows that we are sinful by nature and left to ourselves we will do evil, and thus deserve punishment. Grace, however, does what we cannot do. It gives us eternal life that we do not deserve and gives us God's Spirit to help us do good things. Anyone who is hoping in karma for a good life now or in the future should flee to Jesus Christ for His gift of grace.

Inside every man's soul is a deep wound that he has carried throughout the aeons of time. A karma of lifetimes of an inherent link to the ones who defied God and fell from grace. So based on the aforementioned information, you may believe in reincarnation of having lived in some other form of nature in past lives and enter this one with good or bad karma you had not yet dealt with. So in that belief, it is for you to face up to and deal with these karmic forces in the here and now, and if not then that carries on to your future life after death and a new reincarnation. Conversely, you may have a Christian belief of not so much past life karma cleansing but present life experience of a deep wound of original sin inherited from our human ancestry, and wrong doing throughout one's own life, for which you can only make amends by embracing God's love through The Christ Jesus. i.e.In the acknowledgment of one's defects of character in prayer and sacrifice. In acceptance of being forgiven and cleansed into the light of faith through the "Grace of God" and the Holy Spirit we are freed from past karma and can live a good karmic life henceforth. Knowing also that one day you may face judgement and the consequences of your life in the next one is a driving force of acceptance to adhere to this belief. It's a forward thinking belief of tomorrow's land and not of past bad karma for Christians and equally believers of a life hereafter of other faiths. It would be remiss of me not to consider the concepts of belief of karma, grace and reincarnation in other non christian religious philosophy before examining the workings of such doctrines of faith and morals for the benefit of all.

Whilst philosophies of Buddhism, and the major denominations of Hinduism (Vaishnavism, Shaivism, Shaktism and Smarta) and Sikhism use various sources of their traditions in the laws of karma and eternal truth, it must be noted that there is also a strong tradition to question authority inorder to deepen the understanding of their particular belief and to further develop their tradition and practices. Unlike Christians who believe literally in the written word of the Bible of Old or New Testaments as fact and not just stories that have unfolded over time for our betterment. For there is an inherent danger in carrying into actions some biblical written questionable truths resulting in bad karmic outcomes for the individual or humanity at large. Equally those of Muslim faith who believe in the literal written words of Mohammad's Quaranic teaching of essential significance to understanding. Not to miss the key to an understanding of Judaism, for its primal affirmations appear in early historical narratives. Thus, the Bible reports contemporary events and activities for essentially religious reasons. The biblical authors believed that the divine presence is encountered primarily within history. God's presence is also experienced within the natural realm, but the more immediate or intimate disclosure occurs in human actions. Although other ancient communities also perceived a divine presence in history, the understanding of the ancient Israelites proved to be the most lasting and influential.

It is this particular claim—to have experienced God's presence in human events—and its subsequent development that is the differentiating factor in Jewish thought. Jewish people believe in karma so to speak. The Yin-yang of natural outcomes?

"Since our biological evolution is the foundation of our existence, the purpose of our lives is to "evolve" during our lifetime by learning and growing. Each day our purpose is to strive to be a little bit better than the day before and to continue to evolve throughout our lifetime."

-The Philosopher.

CHAPTER 2

THE WORKINGS OF REINCARNATION

Reincarnation if you will was a hotbed of controversy during the Second Temple Period (515BC-70BC) before the expectation of the coming of a Saviour King. The Pharisees, members of a Jewish religious party at the time, hotly debated their belief in an afterlife, whereas the Sadducees, who belonged to the aristocracy and the priestly class, saw no need for a resurrection to solve problems of the vindication of divine providence in view of the existence of evil. They supposed that all our actions are in our own power, so that we ourselves are the causes of what is good and receive what is evil from our own folly. Interestingly, this view closely resembles the Greek philosophy of the Epicureans; the hedonist of that time of sexual pleasures. There is no text of the Sadducees sect other than several biblical references to support their belief which appears in Job, Ecclesiastes and the Wisdom of Jesus, which harmonise well with their philosophy. For the Sadducees knew that when the Bible is interpreted literally, there is scant evidence for an afterlife. I am not referring here to New Testament teaching but the old biblical ones for Christ who was not even born at the time.

According to Flavius Josephus, (c 37-c 100) [Jewish historian, revolutionary leader, and a Pharisee,] Jewish and the New Testament writings, the Pharisees were the dominant religious force of the Second Temple Period which evolved into Rabbinic Judaism after the destruction of the Jewish temple during the reign of suffering souls of the Babylon period. They returned to the promised land to rebuild their lives and a second temple, and a new surge of religious faith to the word of God emerged. They were strong believers in a bodily resurrection but they may also have been influenced by the Greek followers of Plato's philosophy (Platonist) who had the notion that the soul was immortal. They believed that the soul would leave the body at the time of death and exist independently from the body. However, they held that the soul would return to the body at the time of resurrection in order to be judged as one unified entity at the great judgement. Unlike karma-belief, theirs was that the soul left the body at the time of death and the world lived independently with no need for future resurrection because the good or a bad soul would receive its just reward. This parallels the views of the Platonic immortality of the soul concept.

According to the writings of Josephus, the ancient Jewish sect believed in the immortality of the soul and it was the Jewish religious group most closely related to the Platonic afterlife belief. Considering all literature of the time, it is apparent that there is no progress from a basic to a more complex death and resurrection view as multiple levels of complexity present through this period. Thus, there is no linear development of the resurrection belief, rather multiple views co-existed, although a theological concern with death and the final destiny of the soul, judgement bodily afterlife was ever present for both Rabbinic Judaism and the early Christian

Church. During the Second Temple Period, there were multiple views on life after death developed independently within different faith communities. Thus, there was no obvious progression where earlier beliefs were expanded and built upon later beliefs. The common factor between most of the then eighteen complete beliefs and numerous partial beliefs appearing in Biblical or related writings and the pseudonymous writings, especially Jewish writings, ascribed to various biblical patriarchs and prophets composed within some 200 years before the birth of Christ. By the end of the Second Temple Period, the resurrection belief had become the orthodox view among the two surviving branches of Judaism. In Rabbinic Judaism, resurrection was taken for granted, and it was argued that the resurrection belief was founded on Hebrew scripture. In early Christianity, the focus was placed on Jesus's resurrection from the dead as the foundation for the belief that His followers will also experience a final destiny of the soul on resurrection.

Natural life is cyclical. Day fades into night and turns back into day as the sun rises. One season gradually gives way to the next. Over the passage of time, new generations are born and old ones die. The continuous succession of birth, death and rebirth permeates nature even though our own lives seem linear. So it's no surprise that some ancient observers looked at the seeming linearity of human existence and decided that life, like the natural world, might actually be more cyclical than linear. Multiple religions, philosophies and movements adopted this belief in cyclic life, or reincarnation. It is also called trans-migration or metempsychosis, the concept that the soul, or some aspect of the soul is reborn into new lives. Depending on the religion or philosophy, the soul can appear incarnate in humans, animals or plants as it works its way toward an eventual escape from the cycle of birth, death and rebirth. Most religions that believe in reincarnation consider it the path to purity and salvation. Reincarnation is widely accepted by the major Eastern religions -- most prominently Hinduism and Buddhism. It also has a history in ancient Greek philosophy. However, for people more familiar with the major monotheistic religions -- Christianity, Judaism and Islam -- the idea of eastern type reincarnation seems foreign and maybe even a little strange. That's because Christianity, Judaism and Islam conceive of time linearly. Life is simply a short step that determines the quality of an afterlife. For those who believe in only one life followed by an eternal afterlife, reincarnation is like an unwieldy marathon run by relay instead of a short, concise sprint.

The Hindu religion is vast and varied. Its adherents worship an array of Gods and celebrate diverse traditions. Yet Hinduism, the world's oldest surviving religion, is unified by its acceptance of samsara, a chain of births and deaths linked by reincarnation. Controlling samsara is the law of karma. Hindus believe that all individuals accumulate karma over the course of a lifetime. Good actions create good karma and evil actions create negative karma. Karma is not assigned or regulated by any God; it's simply earned by an individual and passed down through subsequent lives.

But while good karma can eventually earn a person a higher place in the caste system in a future life, the ultimate goal of any Hindu adherent is moksha, or salvation from samsara. Moksha is the final of four primary Hindu goals. The first three- karma the God of love, the essence or purpose of love and dharma, the eternal law of the cosmos concern earthly pursuits like pleasure, power or well-being and virtue. Ironically, to achieve the ultimate goal of moksha, you must make a deliberate effort to not want it. Salvation comes only after a person has abandoned all pursuits and desires and accepts that the individual soul is the same as Brahman, the universal soul or God. By exiting the cycle, an individual no longer endures the pain and suffering of earthly existence performed countless times over.

Hindus believe the soul is trapped in a circle of birth and rebirth samsara. Until a person quells desires and accepts that the individual soul is the same as the absolute soul, he or she must suffer in samsara and forgo Moksha- the goal of salvation. But because Moksha is an ultimate goal, and one that can be achieved only after it is no longer desired, most Hindus attempt to generate good karma so that they can be born into a better life. The law of karma controls samsara, with good actions engendering good karma and bad actions creating negative karma, good karma is usually produced by correctly performing the duties of one's caste, or social class. If a person lives admirably and fulfils the responsibilities of the caste, the soul can be reborn into a higher caste. Hindus also believe that because karma is its own law, it requires no divine interference.

While most Hindus believe that an unchanging soul is reincarnated until it achieves salvation, Buddhists believe that a soul accumulates karma, rather than the soul itself transmigrating between bodies. Buddhists don't believe in a soul in the Western sense; instead, they believe in a soul-like compilation of attributes. The soul, which consists of the five strands of clinging aggregates of body, sensations, perceptions, impulses and consciousness- expires at death. However, the soul's accumulated karma becomes the "germ of consciousness" in a new life [source: Encyclopaedia Britannica]. Like Hindus, Buddhists strive to escape the cycles of samsara by achieving a stage of complete passiveness. Many Buddhist believe that individuals can end the cycle of reincarnation and achieve "nirvana" by passing through multiple lifetimes following the Eightfold (obey) Path or the"middle way." More will be revealed about the Eightfold Path and "nirvana" in the process of this chapter.

Belief in reincarnation is also predominant in two prevalent religions from India: Jainism and Sikhism. Jain adherents believe the soul's accumulate karma as an actual physical substance, unlike the conceptual Hindu idea of karmic law. As long as the soul is burdened by karmic particles, it must bind with a body, initiating a series of rebirths.

Only when a soul is free from all karma can it exit the cycle of reincarnation and join other disembodied souls in a state of perfection. However, because Jain followers believe that deliverance is currently impossible, devoted adherents simply pursue purification. Sikhism also teaches reincarnation. Like Hinduism, the law of karma influences the quality of Sikh life. For Sikhs to exit the cycle of birth and rebirth, they must achieve complete knowledge and become one with God.

When Buddhism was established 2,500 years ago, it incorporated the Hindu belief in reincarnation. Although Buddhism has two major subdivisions and countless variations in regional practices, most Buddhists believe in samsara or the cycle of rebirth. Samsara is governed by the law of karma: Good conduct produces good karma and bad conduct produces evil karma. Buddhists believe that the soul's karma transmigrates between bodies and becomes a "germ of consciousness" in the womb [source: Encyclopaedia Britannica]. Periods of afterlife, sometimes called "the between," punctuate samsara, coming after death and before rebirth [source: NPR]. Like Hindus, Buddhists see unenlightened samsara as a state of suffering. We suffer because we desire the transient. Only when we achieve a state of total passiveness and free ourselves from all desire can we escape samsara and achieve nirvana, or salvation. Many Buddhists believe an individual can end the cycle of reincarnation by following the Eightfold Path, or middle way. An enlightened being embodies the directives of the Eightfold Path: of correct view, intention, speech, action, livelihood, effort, mindfulness and concentration.

The Buddha Siddhartha Gautama taught the Eightfold Path in his first sermon after attaining enlightenment. Siddhartha, who was born around 563 B.C. near modern-day Nepal, had an extravagant and privileged youth. As a young man, he began to question his spiritual state amid such luxury and reverted to the life of an extreme ascetic. When his hermetic life brought him no closer to enlightenment, Siddhartha decided to pursue the middle way-a state of existence between excess and self-deprivation. Soon Siddhartha reached enlightenment. Although reincarnation seems conventional to the more than 1.25 billion practitioners of Hinduism and Buddhism, it's not widely accepted by those outside of Eastern religion. The Western **style** of reincarnation monotheistic religions focus on a single life, a single soul and an active God who does not rely on karmic law (with sporadic believers announcing they're Cleopatra or Elvis reincarnate) It is not surprising many people remain extremely aware of the soul's ability to return repeatedly. Although belief in reincarnation is a predominant element of many Eastern religions, it also was taught in the ancient Western world. Mystery religions, which sometimes transformed into secularised social clubs or fraternities, espoused a wide range of reincarnation ceremonies and beliefs. Some of these early Greco-Roman religions eventually influenced the philosophy of famous thinkers like Plato.

Orphism was a popular mystery religion beginning in the sixth or seventh century B.C. Its followers studied the supposed writings of Orpheus, a legendary musical figure. They believed in a soul that withstood death and could appear incarnate in human or mammalian form. Orphic's thought the soul was divine and was imprisoned by the body. By leading a correct life and abstaining from meat, wine and sex, a soul could go to Elysium, a paradise after death; an evil soul would suffer punishments in hell. But neither afterlife was eternal and after a time, the soul would be reborn into a new body. Only after passing through three good Orphic lives could a soul end the cycle of reincarnation. The Orphic interest in death and the afterlife influenced the Pythagorean brotherhood, another mystery society based in southern Italy. The philosopher and mathematician Pythagoras, who is associated with the brotherhood, believed the soul could appear incarnate in a human or animal's body. This belief led to his espousal of vegetarianism. The fraternity taught that the soul originated among the stars but fell to earth and joined with the human body. Pythagorean followers combined their religious theorising with the studies of astronomy, music and, of course, geometry.

The philosopher Plato also believed that the soul was repeatedly reincarnated. Plato suspected that seven planetary spheres and an eighth sphere of fixed stars surrounded the Earth. The divine lay beyond the eighth sphere and set the universe into motion. Souls came from the planets, descended to earth, united with bodies and then tried to free themselves and reascend to the stars. A hope of eternal rest in a happy heavenly space. In most modern religious funeral services, be they of Christian, Jewish or other denominations, a word to the Almighty God is said: "May he/ she rest in peace." It may be determined as rest in the bosom of the Almighty, rest in the heavenly kingdom or just be at peace in a hereafter free from the valley of tears here on earth, a transcendent stage relieved from earthly woes or whatever it is that floats one's boat in a spirit of passing over.

You probably hear the word "nirvana" pretty often. People might say they've achieved nirvana when they're really happy, or they might talk about going to nirvana as an eternal reward after death.. The word "nirvana" is fully entrenched in modern vocabulary. But do you know what it actually means? To most people in the Western world, religious nirvana is a total mystery. If you don't know much about Eastern religion, you'll probably be surprised at what nirvana actually is. Nirvana is a transcendent state in which there is neither suffering, desire, nor sense of self, and the subject is released from the effects of karma and the cycle of death and rebirth. It represents the final goal of Buddhism. It used to refer to the extinction of desire, hatred and, ultimately, of suffering and rebirth. Literally it means 'blowing out" or becoming extinguished like the flame of a candle.

However, the idea of karma is still appealing to people unfamiliar with eastern roots. Karma suggests that self determination is possible and that actions can influence the future quality of one's life, be that in the present, earthly future or in the hereafter. Karma has become a popular New Age ethical philosophy- one largely removed from religious connotations. The simple ethical basis, that good engenders good and visa versa- translates into most religions. The popularised doctrine of karma started in the West in part with the creation of the Theosophical Society in the late 19th century. Russian immigrant/ defector to the USA, Helena Blavatsky founded the society with Henry Steel Olcott, a lawyer and journalist, in 1875 in New York City. Blavatsky originally shaped the group's doctrine around gnostic mystical knowledge and the kabbalah, ancient Jewish traditions of mystical interpretations of the Bible. But in 1879 on a trip to India she was attracted to Hinduism and a more regimented understanding of karma. Blavatsky believed that the Theosophical Society's studies, discussions and mediations could help prepare the world for the Aquarian Age, using ancient wisdom to a time of enlightenment and brotherhood. An English devotee, Annie Besant, helped extend the society's reach and introduced modified Hindu beliefs to the West. Today the society defines karma as "a law of spiritual dynamics related to every act in daily life." It is a view of karma that is only loosely connected to the structure of Hindu, Buddhist, Sikh or Jain philosophies.

So, it is that I was contemplating the words I had written some two decades ago of my karmic fall from a world of what I had perceived to be my destiny. It proved to be the cathartic miracle of a new direction in my life that has worked out for the better despite the downward spiral that I had expected. I am going to relate it for your benefit and understanding in the hope that it grants you some benefit to know what the experience of travelling through bad karma, living good karma incorporation of co-creative thought through the God of my own understanding intimately grants me grace.

I had come to a mystical side of myself that could not be expressed in words or through worldly deeds; a cause that could be fulfilled only by the spirit that was central to the candle that burned within - a candle that to me was a symbol of life itself, a flame that burned at a deep level, projecting light into the darkness. And in the flickering awareness I could almost hear a message: "Exist; stay alive; survive." Here, for the first time, I was learning about my true nature, aware of my body, my mind and the true spirit within. I had come from a darkness and had tried to clutch too tightly to the past when my worldly concerns engulfed me. Yet here I was now, surrendering my all, falling moment by moment into that surrendering and risking falling into the unknown; falling into the fearful dragon's mouth of self-acceptance, with the fear of falling into a pit of darkness where the dragon lived, where there was no light, only darkness, of weeping and gnashing of teeth. It was there that I had fallen part of the way previously, when I lost all that I thought life was about. Wife, children, friends, business and wealth had left me, and it was then that I had turned to other lovers; lovers who brought me their pain in my pain, comfort in my agony, illusion in their mystic lover-rites. I'd had a sense of the Goddess for a brief moment, only to find disenchantment and, once more, illusion. A cover of the inner truth that I was seeing clearly now for the first time in my life. I had turned to regain the respect of my children only to find that they had moved on, as was their right. All I could do now was to be there for them in the event of their fall; be there now, in a sober mind. I had struggled to regain the wealth that I once possessed, only to find that apart from the need for food, clothing and shelter, the pursuit of wealth was of little comfort to me. I felt apart from the world I once knew and was coming to realise that my heart no longer craved for anything that was once my sure-fire way of enthusiasm for living. I had taken an inner-truth of honesty to myself; an open-mindedness and a willingness to grow; a willingness not to worry; of acceptance; of belief in living with whatever comes my way. I began to relax then, to allow the coil of the wound-up spring within me to slowly unwind, let-go and trust in God without definition. I knew it was not the old ways of strength, enthusiasm, leadership and dogma that would project me like an arrow towards some designated target. Rather, it was to be a slow road, one day at a time, moment to moment to moment, using the spiritual thread of the coiled spring to unwind, unravel and let-go in order to achieve inner calm. I was learning to use no force, to let the force within take hold, allowing time to heal and grow, I knew I needed to go with the grain, as an artist working with wood in time knows. Often in the past I had run against the grain and the result was splintered wounds. I was running now with the flow of the inner river and was going with the current in open water. I knew that once I understood and accepted the drift of it, a gentle movement of the rudder would keep me on course!

On previous falls into the pit I had taken a parachute of meaningless clutched possessions and wild ego notions; a crutch to lessen the impact of the fall. The residual inner nervous tension had remained, and so this time I was going without a parachute, without forethought, without a plan. I knew that I had to just be to win; to give way to keep; to surrender to get well; to die to live! So the new life of the inner spiritual was unfolding. I was learning to let-go and allow the inner core of my being to take hold of something from nothingness.

It was where I now believed the universe began: that something that was my God. I discovered within myself a way of cutting through to the reality of everything that comprised my life, and an enlightened ability to judge and act with wisdom; discovered, symbolically, a 'Sword of Discernment,' a tool to carry as my staff of action, my brand of reason. I had a choice now: to use my discernment sword like a knight of old, to just go with the flow, nice and easy, and accept with free will whatever comes along; to use my inner discernment with wisdom and understanding whenever and wherever I may think fit; to pursue or not to pursue in consideration of who and what I was beginning to realise I was, am and will be; the right to act or not to act according to the dictates of my consciousness, of my heart and the beauty that lived within me.

I had determined to adopt an accord of consciousness with every human being with whom I would come in contact on my outward and inward journey: a journey of understanding; a journey of nature being both cruel and kind; of being as vigilant as a female serpent within my inner being on the pathways of my life, and as innocent as a dove. A freedom nothing bar death could take from me – my freedom of choice for living. I knew within my heart of hearts there existed a Sword of Discernment and I longed for, an outward expressive symbol of this inner need and courage. I would venture forth, to let-go of my inner turmoil and take a journey of the spirit–my spiritual heart expressed in a real symbol. I could think of no better way than the way of St. James, the Apostle, whose symbol was a real Sword of Discernment; the sacrificial cross of St. James, the fleury fitch, whose sword blade signifies the sword of a warrior. I would follow the path of St. James, the Moor-slayer, on The Camino Way, where I would lay-down my burdens and walk the traditional Way that so many pilgrims had walked before me. I felt that I knew the outward expression of that which I sought would manifest into the sword of St. James. Like the Spanish who fought and conquered the Moors so many centuries ago, their vision of the Saint on a white steed advancing before them holding aloft a fiery red sword of Santiago, leading their charge and taking them to victory. I, likewise, would venture forth on the road to Santiago, leading ever onward with a courageous cry, to the quest that pierced my heart. I would walk The Camino de Santiago. Whilst I would seek a symbolic sword as proof of my journey, I knew that my 'Sword of Discernment' would be more than merely a sword. I knew I would express in words the cry of my heart, the link that I had to my past journey. My current turmoil would be in my spiritual quest. I would venture forth with hope and confidence despite the dark night of the soul. I did not yet know the events that would unfold as a result of walking my Camino. The thought of a new dawning after the long night gave me courage to step forth. The night is darkest just before the dawning and, despite the sword that pierced my soul, I ventured forth.

Looking back now after my fall from grace I had time to reflect on my part entering into a period of what to me at the time seemed to be bad karma. There was for many years of my life a period of good karma in the growth of my family tree, in the love of a dutiful wife, the pursuit of the education of my children and the getting of wisdom in business affairs. Over many decades I amassed great wealth, devoted myself to exploring many things, undertook great projects, learnt the art of buying and selling and taught others through my experience. However, I had forgotten how to be grateful, enjoyed far to many pleasures to my own liking, and was driven more by six of the seven deadly sins of pride, covertness, lust, anger, gluttony, envy, but not so much of sloth; for I was far too busy with the process of making money to drift into habits of laziness.

I was living life in the fast lane on an ever revolving spinning wheel like a ferret in a cage. I seemed to be running to stand still. My only relief was the pleasure of drinking copious amounts of wine at the end of each day to unwind. It seemed the only relief for all that I was striving for. Life and love had lost meaning and purpose for me. The thought of praying to God for guidance never entered my head, instead I just took on more responsibilities and drove myself even harder, existed on limited sleep and had deceived myself into thinking I was happy and showed love in my heart. In truth, I provided service with a smile but love was not the mantra that I was living nor preaching. Then came the great falling. A series of personal tragedies that seemed to engulf me drove me further to drink. In the space of a year I had lost my wife and family, and a cherished son who died by his own hand. A series of further misfortunes over the twelve month period that followed brought me to rack and ruin. In that period, I went through many calamities that I could not find a way out of and copious quantities of alcohol seemed to be my only friend for a time. I fell into deep despair and collapsed into the darkest of places in my mind, hid in the bush in desolation of spirit. It was when at the lowest ebb of my downward decline that I cried out for help… and God slowly granted me a new direction. It seems to come first through walking the Camino de Santiago where I discovered on my first journey how to let go and let God guide me. For I had come to understand that I was powerless over my circumstances. I had discovered that a power greater than self was guiding me to His light. That the fearful dragon's mouth at the bottom of my pit of despair that I fell into, turned into a lotus flower of creative ideas.

Returning from that first Camino of letting go of the old ways and embracing the new, the good karma of a new dawn of creation lay before me. In my enthusiasm and zest for life, I once more threw myself into many projects, wrote books, recorded songs and began to build a business again. I had not yet learnt the lesson of harnessing my eccentricities. The recognition that my ego is like a grain of sand on the beach that is always in danger of thinking its the beach had not yet taken hold. Sure I realise over time that the ego has its place in human progress but it's not to be left in charge. I was soon to learn that it was my logical linear half brain ego notion that ultimately caused my fall from good karma and Godly grace.

So it was in my wild erratic fantasies, in my writing, my songs and numerous projects that I had taken on board, that I found myself in utter exhaustion and back in rehabilitation once again. The only good thing that had emerged from this lesson of betterment was that I had stopped drinking alcohol and had regained my self worth. The belief that I didn't run the show had dawned again, so I began to immerse myself into the programme of Alcoholics Anonymous.

However, the old ways of the flesh and feelings of unfilled needs returned. So, mistakenly I returned to the arms of a woman instead of running to the greater good of the 'Son of the Father' for help and guidance. In this new search I returned once more to a Camino journey. There I fell into the entrapment of the lust of a beautiful woman but it was destined for failure, for I had once again mistaken lust for love. No good karma for me came from that encounter, for on my return home I once more fell into the hole of depression and loss of confidence in God. Many months later I emerged from hospitalisation after much mental torment and loss of a will to live. I returned to work once again, a sadder but wiser man by all accounts from friends and work associates. I can't remember much of the next year but somehow with God's good orderly direction and much body rest I did recover.

" Deep down in every man, woman and child is a fundamental idea of God.
It may be obscured by calamity, by prompt, by worship of other things, but in some form or another it is there. For faith in a 'Power greater than ourselves,' and miraculous demonstration of that Power in human lives are a fact as old as man himself."

- As Bill sees it. Page 152. Bill Wilson, AA Co-founder.

CHAPTER 3

KARMIC FALL TO GRACE

The fall of the winter in Europe was early that year, but something in my heart was magnetically attracting me back to Spain to walk yet another Camino. It is fine to be wise in hindsight but to set forth once more without a map or spiritual compass to guide me, lost in some mental wilderness, was insane. Physically I was far from ready for the ordeal that awaited me but this time I had no agenda. I wanted to do it for myself. A man in a sorry state of recovery trying to break the spell of prescription drugs to alleviate depression, a serious bacterial infection coupled with an irritating skin ailment that modern medicine had no answer to, and sick with influenza, I set forth. To the logical brain it was sheer madness, but I believed then that there was something aligned in the spirit of the universe which would change everything for me. A hunch came to mind that this pilgrimage would be more than just a hard tramp, it would be a spiritual path back to health physically, mentally and spiritually. Somewhere deep inside I was yearning for a miracle of sorts to happen for me, or maybe I was seeking a new direction in a renewal of faith; a guiding light to show me the way through the darkness. Thinking about the pilgrimage some five years later, perhaps I just needed to tramp the hills and valleys of foreign shores, to get my sense of worth and spiritual balance back intact.

It took me a couple of hours to pack my essentials for the journey. Using my past journeys' rule of thumb, I had determined that 7 kilos of all weather gear, medical kit, sleeping bag, head lamp and sundry would be adequate for what lay ahead. This proved to be the exact weight on the airport scales as I boarded the plane. I marvelled at the miracles of the universe, as I had not pre checked the bag weight when I packed it. On the previous Camino journeys in both Spain and Portugal I struck fair weather, hot and dry conditions which I relished as ideal. However, this journey proved to be just the opposite to what I had previously encountered. It rained continuously for the next month. Most nights I did my best to dry my clothing by a fireplace or draped over the end of the bunk I happened to crawl into from time to time along the way. As for my boots they never seemed to dry, soaked inside and out and covered in mud mostly. I endured these conditions of being wet, cold and weary for the majority of days on this journey. Despite my physical discomforts and lack of adequate gear for the ever present cold weather, I was of good spirit. I completed that walk having beaten depression, free of prescription drugs and alcohol. My skin irritation had not improved and the chest infection was still a discomfort but I felt strong enough to continue my pilgrim progress.

The desire to visit Ireland, the homeland of my ancestors, had taken hold. So I landed in Dublin and headed by bus to the Wicklow Way. Despite its proximity to Dublin, the Wicklow Mountains offered me hundreds of kilometres of wonderfully unspoilt trails and a wide variety of scenic landscapes. So it was that in what proved unusually warm sunny days, I climbed the mountains, walked near upland lakes, traversed steep sided glacial valleys, refreshed my spirit in fast flowing mountain streams, and breathed the forest air with the sounds of nature attuned to my soul. It was 131 km of the Wicklow Way, crossing the Wicklow Mountains from south to north, through the village of Clonegal in County Carlow to Marlay Park, returning to the suburbs of Dublin. I had taken it all , that which nature had to offer and marvelled at the green earth of Irish farmland too. I wrote many poems on that journey, touched the void so to speak in the corners of my mind, but as yet I had not got the wonder lust out of my system. So I ventured on, crossed to the Aran Islands, riding a push bike one way and tramping the rest on foot. Then back on the mainland I set forth on the Burren Way near Galway in wet and freezing conditions. I had journeyed 1200 kilometres before nature and reason returned and I headed back home to Australia. I had tramped my way inward but it took months to recover from my marathon effort. I did manage to write two more books and record another album of songs as an aftermath of my journey. Despite the ordeal, the sufferings endured, I did come out the other side with internal fortitude and karmic experience for my betterment. So I can now look at it not as the output of a man who lost his way, but more than that one who found a gem inside a pearl of great price.

I now know that my past life had me heavily entrapped into the karma of the same old patterns that pulled towards all types of people, work, events, and unneeded burdens. So for what it's worth to you and as a further reminder to me, let me express the way to free the soul of bad karma. Unlike the physical burden of my backpack on my pilgrimages, Karma is the luggage the soul carried on its trip from life to life. Unfortunately, unlike luggage at the airport, this particular baggage never gets lost, which means we are stuck with it until one opens it up and sorts through its ancient contents. Without even knowing it, we may be experiencing karma that originated several lifetimes ago. But when we do dig through the karmic suitcase, then finally, we can confront outstanding karma and lighten the energetic load. That's why it's important to acknowledge the role of each person in one's life: Why are they there? What have they come to teach you and vice versa? What is the karma you're meant to experience with this person? The sooner we acknowledge the truth of the karma we share with someone (be it good or bad), the sooner we can settle it. We often think of karma as "what goes around comes around." But the reality of karma is more than just being "punished" for our bad deeds—positive karma exists just as much as negative karma. If you steal, others will steal from you in following lives. If you nourish, you will be nourished.

One of the most fascinating facts about karma is that it often causes us to reincarnate in a reversed manner. This means that your parent may have actually been your child in a former life. Then, before reincarnating in this lifetime, the souls agreed to take on the opposite act. Souls switch gender too. Positions shift throughout lifetimes based on karmic need, whatever dynamic is needed to repair or heal karma will be manifested through changing roles in our cycle of lives on earth. The people you know now may have had a very different time and experience in previous lives to help you. There's a greater reason that karma repeats itself, and it's not to cause you pain. Instead, it's to teach you to take different actions for different results. If you're attracting the same type of partners into your life over and over again, it's time to stop and inspect your choices: Why do similar people keep coming in? What should you be doing differently? This calls for honest introspection and evaluation of your own faults and weaknesses, which is admittedly hard to do. Don't be afraid to look within. Recognise what must be changed inside of you so as to change what's outside of you. Then you can modify your behaviour to end karmic patterns and progress in your potential. Past-life karma is resoundingly present in your current life. Mustering up the courage to open your karmic suitcase today can change your destiny for lifetimes to come.

So it is that in my present state I am bound to a unique karma that I need to unlock to dispel any unwanted circumstances. This is part and parcel with my reason for now writing a dissertation here. To date, I have not been willing to free fall unto that karma void without a residual parachute to support me into the dragon's mouth of soul experience to lighten my fall so to speak. I have used writing books, recording songs and anything but having the courage to suffer the pain of the experience of free fall. Formally I used alcohol, sex, work and worldly goals and aspirations to do this. Anything but having the courage to face it once and for all. I now realise I needed to pinpoint the areas in my life to reverse the karma of stagnation. Is it not herein implicit to reflect honestly on obstacles and understand where the problem lies? Yes, it is essential to untangle my karmic knots and advance towards my true potential to get to the root of what blocks my spiritual progress.

An ever present example is the reason I ventured on writing this book in the first place. This book is, if I am being truthful, another residual parachute which must be faced as fact in my present task. There are many ties with toxic people from the past that, whilst I have freed myself of association with them by my choice or theirs, I am yet to grant myself the willingness to confess either face to face or indirectly in writing, honest admission of my part in causing bad karma in their lives. Once I take this action, keep my ego in check, and let them know that I am sorry for the hurt I may have caused, then I shall not be free of the bad karma. Free to absorb only good karmic experience as a positive outcome. It is also essential that I set boundaries in doing so in order to defend my soul, self and spirit from further complications or attracting the flack of their own bad karma. Then again, I also have to consider if I am opening up old wounds for those I wish to make amends. This takes some reasoning for it may be better to just make amends in writing or in prayerful meditation confession alone in lieu of face to face confrontation or posting a letter of contrition. Thus, hastening slowly is the key to progress for me now.

Just the thought of the admission of my wrongdoing is beginning to lift my energy and uncover a doorway of opportunity to walk through in the process. My ego is crying out for recognition in my intention and I am being warned herein to keep it in check. It is apparent that I must seek my good karmic self and the spirit of grace through prayer and meditation before I set forth with my decision herein. I have within me my inner child to comfort in the process, my bodily self to work good discipline too. It now seems necessary to renew my energy source by eating nourishing food, doing more regular exercise, getting plenty of sleep and taking time out to sit quietly and self reflect before venturing to set my plan to action on a spiritual level. I can no longer become the victim of vulnerabilities for this would invite a sort of karmic scenario that will play on my sensitivities. I must defy my previous downfalls and take the reins of karmic patterns. I can now see that I must slow down enough to notice if my old ways of doing things aren't beneficial anymore. If they're not, then it's time to modify my behaviour. There is an old saying: 'when in doubt act in ways you would want others to act towards you.' And another comes to mind: 'When in doubt communicate.' We often wonder why we can't escape the wheel of negativity. It is because we avoid the truth that it's our very emotions that reel us into such cycles of behaviour. To forgive is to detach from anger, bitterness and the frustrations we harbour internally. Every person is fighting his or her own karmic battles. The sooner we identify the sources of our unsettled karma and take action to resolve it, the sooner we experience the miracle of liberation to fulfil the greater purpose of our lives as God has ordained for us in the present.

Firstly comes pain and then much suffering before the miracle of good karma and grace transpires. To begin changing our understanding of pain and suffering, we must firstly consider what pain really is. There's physical pain, of course. But there's also mental and emotional pain. Just as physical pain is designed to notify us when something is wrong, so is emotional pain. If we're having chest pain or achy joints, we take it as a signal to reach out for help. We know something needs attention. Likewise, emotional pain is our brain's way of telling us that something important needs to be addressed. But the emotional discomfort we feel often drives us to find ways to avoid it or ignore it. Rather than look at the underlying causes for our pain, we choose to focus on the unpleasant way it makes us feel. Sometimes we get caught up in negativity and complaining when we spend too much time focusing on the source of our pain. We can let anger overtake us at the unfairness of our situation. Maybe we dwell on how hard things are for us. Unfortunately, these reactions only prolong the pain—and create suffering. For this is what suffering is. When we ignore our pain and get angry about it, we allow suffering to invade our lives. We create suffering in our lives by what we do with the difficulties we encounter.

So it was that many calamities led to my fall from grace, too much physical pain and suffering, mental torment and exhaustion before I began the slow uphill progress on the road to recovery. It came through the depths of depression, a necessary precursor to my recovery back to mental and physical health. Spiritual recovery, as it does by our very nature, takes a longer pathway to recovery and enlightenment. It's an ongoing pilgrimage to a world without end, so it seems. When I had the awakening to the will of a God of my own understanding, I had been lost and bewildered. First came creative output of stories and songs that I was inspired to write as I tramped my happy path of destiny. However, the danger was that I let my old self determine outcomes. For I was under the delusion that this new found gift of being, for want of a better word 'a wordsmith,' was to be my future worldly lifestyle. For far too long I used creative output as my means to recovery. It has proven just another residual parachute to mask pain and suffering in letting go to the spiritual self ordained by God. Falling once more into the dragon's mouth of a lotus flower of creative output, I had once again mistakenly used my books and songs as the means to spirituality. The world rewards my efforts in this regard and my ego delights in the applause, but it's a false God that I have experienced and not the truth of my designated path inward. Not that I will stop writing for the process is cathartic but it is not the way of the spirit for me, that is altogether a different journey. My spiritual pathway I am discovering now is more through the healing power of the steps of Alcoholics Anonymous, the renewal to meditation, good diet, exercise, rest and recreation.

Many people will do anything they can to avoid dealing with their emotional pain. They try to silence their emotions with food, alcohol, drugs, sex, or work as I had done. When uncomfortable feelings popped up, I ran away from them and resisted them with those artificial comforters instead of turning to God for guidance. It is nature's way to learn to stop suffering when we actually choose to stay open to our pain and carefully listen to what it is trying to tell us. We don't have to let our pain make us angry. We don't have to expend negative emotional energy trying to avoid it. Instead, we can learn to observe our pain, examine our expectations and beliefs, and choose to believe that it will pass. Training ourselves to realise that emotions are fleeting and temporary is an important step in saying no to suffering. Like anything in life, it's not a once-and-done change. Altering our perspective on the pain experience and what to do with it is an ongoing journey. It takes practice. As we go through different painful situations and experiences, we may need to go deeper into analysing our reactions. As with any skill, the more we practise, the more skilled we become.

Whilst I know I have come a long way on the physical and emotional level of letting go of the experiences of being hurt, I am reminded of the fact that when emotional pain prevents me from healing from a situation, it's a sign that I am not moving forward in a growth-oriented way. So it is just a matter of looking back at what propelled me forward to where I am now by trimming the sails of my boat of personality back on the spiritual waters of life. Once the course is reset, it is just a matter of a slight touch of the rudder to stay on course. Often, in the past it was having a positive mantra to tell me in times of emotional pain to reframe my thoughts. A simple: "Not my will but thine be done," as a mantra will work as has the AA serenity prayer: "God grant me the serenity. To accept the things I cannot change; Courage to change the things I can; And wisdom to know the difference."

For a long time in my past mantra as a link to the scaffolding of my former belief that I am slowly finding a renewal in, I used to say the mantra:
'Mar- ran- artha' which is an Arabic word meaning in English "Come Lord Jesus, come." The clinical psychologist Carla Manly PhD advocates a positive mantra like: "I am fortunate to be able to find a new path in life — one that is good for me."

Early in my recovery, before I could cope with mental and emotional difficulties due to the various calamities that were instrumental in my fall from grace, I found the bad karma of some people seemed to cling to me to my detriment. In time I learnt to create both a physical and psychological distance between them, creating those boundaries to help with my letting go. In simple terms I did not have to think about them or be reminded of the process of my recovery. I gave myself time to process my wounds, reasoning who and what caused me pain and or what my part was in it all without being forced into the influence of often well meaning people. The focus on self was important for me to address the hurt. So I learnt to focus on who or what caused my pain, and to bring myself back to the present. Then, I began to focus on something that I was grateful for. The more I began to focus on the present moment, the less impact my past or or indeed future had on me. I learnt the more freedom I had to choose how I want to respond to any given situation the better I responded to difficulties. No more criticism for myself now, for I learnt in time to show myself and others some kindness and compassion. "Hurt is inevitable, and we may not be able to avoid pain; however, we can choose to treat ourselves and others kindly and lovingly when it comes."

Many times we are afraid of bad karma such as grief, anger, disappointment, or sadness. Rather than feeling them, people just try to shut them out, which can disrupt the process of letting go. "These negative emotions are like riptides," explains Durvasula. "Let them flow out of you… It may require mental health intervention, but fighting them can leave you stuck," she adds. Waiting for an apology from the person who hurt you will slow down the process of letting go. If you're experiencing hurt and pain, it's important you take care of your own healing, which may mean accepting that the person who hurt you isn't going to apologise. They may be blocked by hurt and pain as a consequence of a past tragedy or an event they prefer to think that they have no responsible part of.

It is easier on the surface to bury the hurt and place blame on another. Such bad karma hangs on to those souls as it does to another. So they may have severe communication problems and everybody associated with the hurt and pain suffer too. When we are hurting, it often feels like there is nothing but hurt. So practising self-care and doing the things that bring joy and comfort,

and listening to our own needs first are the key. I have had a similar experience in my life and now know I have healed to a point of making the approach to resume contact. I can only do this by detachment from the emotional upheaval that may well transpire as a consequence. "The more we can implement self-care into our daily lives, the more empowered we are. From that space, our hurts don't feel as overwhelming, we can move
forward. We can't do life alone, and we can't expect ourselves to get through our hurts alone, either, explains Manly. "Allowing ourselves to lean on loved ones and their support is such a wonderful way of not only limiting isolation but of reminding us of the good that is in our lives."

When you're dealing with painful feelings or a situation that hurts you, it's important to give yourself permission to talk about it. Sometimes people can't let go because they feel they aren't allowed to talk about it. "This may be because the people around them no longer want to hear about it or the person is embarrassed or ashamed to keep talking about it," But talking it out is important. I found sharing at AA, talking with friends who have had the patience to care and writing down my feelings about hurt has made a great deal of difference to my progress in this regard. Since waiting for the other person to apologise can stall the process of letting go, I've had to work on my own forgiveness. And in the process learn to forgive those who have offended me. Forgiveness is vital to the healing process because it allows me to let go of anger, guilt, shame, sadness, or any other feeling I am experiencing to move on. I have in the past resorted to professional help in this regard to help me process the hurt. To let go of past hurts I still need to make the conscious decision to take control of situations. However, this takes time and practice. Be kind to myself as I refocus how I see the situations, and celebrate the small victories I have. It is a blessing towards better karmic outcomes.

The Law of Detachment states that in order to manifest our desires, we must release attachment to the outcome itself as well as the path we might take to get there. "The more we can trust the space between where we are and where we are thinking we should be, the easier life will be." And that means resisting getting triggered by every little challenge or upset. "Take the time to develop a higher state of awareness and we can become aware of the origin of negative emotions and begin to detach from them," The Law of Detachment isn't about not being involved in the world around you or giving up on your goals. "When focusing on what you want, you can energetically strangle the outcome, the moment we detach from how we want an outcome to turn out is when the universe can start getting to work." Co-creation with the universe requires active allowance-as opposed to resistance. Detachment creates space to receive guidance from the universe, that is ultimately the God of your own understanding. It's a simple trust in letting go and allowing things to transpire as they will.

It is said that in nature a seed suffers much as it breaks through the soil to shoot into a beautiful plant or blooms as a flower. As with a baby in the birth canal, it has been proven that the child suffers more in birth pain than the mother does giving birth. It is part and parcel of both mother and child letting go the feelings to nature and the spirit to be in the now. It is a natural human thing to suffer for it is in our lives because we are living in a broken world. Some suffering is due to defects of character and wrongdoing by choice or infliction on others or that another has inflicted suffering on us. Or it may ultimately be that deeper wound that humanity carries as a result of the fall of Lucifer; a piercing pain to the heart of God's ultimate plan of the love of us and for our salvation. Man's suffering because of the rejection of his plan by taking up the gauntlet of the dark side of our world and human nature. The rejection we all stand guilty of in our inheritance from the first man on earth to our present day part in this soul nature. Whatever you perceive it to be, man is destined to suffer and to change in the acceptance and action for our betterment. Although suffering is alien to Godly purposes for humanity, he uses it as part of our development as his people. Nothing forces a person to confront their true self like suffering. It causes our focus to turn inward, to face those workings of ourselves that we may otherwise choose to ignore. God uses suffering to develop us into better people; people who can love and enjoy Him forever (Romans 5:3-5; James 1:2-4). Suffering is the crucible by which we find our centre and demonstrate the truth of our faith to the world. In times of intense pain or turmoil, we cling to what we have placed our hope in. In this way, suffering reveals whether our faith is a mere childish hope or a factual reality. Here we see suffering as a call to live out a better and more faithful witness to the world. Like the prophet Habakkuk, suffering calls us to declare to those around us, "yet I will rejoice in the Lord; I will take joy in the God of my salvation" (Habakkuk 3:18).

CHAPTER 4.

AVATARS OF GOODWILL & GRACE

As we develop an understanding of how to approach suffering, we must be clear that suffering never becomes good. Suffering remains evil. What must be understood though, is that suffering can be redeemed; it can be made purposeful. When we are burdened beyond our strength, we must not become bitter but instead allow our faith to make us better. For the Christian, we must see suffering as a trifold call to long for a better world, to seek to become a better person and to live out a better witness. For those of Islamic belief its the reality of suffering through every endeavour with the ultimate goal of devotion to the Almighty God as related by his Messenger and the Koran teachings. In the Eastern religious philosophies it is travelling life acceptance of the suffering path to Enlightenment as demonstrated by the one who sat under the Bodhi Tree of awakening.

The sufferings of those Avatars of faith accepted their lot not just for their own salvation, but more for the benefit of their fellowman; for it is believed that each knew of their ultimate deathly fate in advance of it eventuating. The Buddha, Jesus and Mohammed it seems were ordained and sent by God in their relevant time to teach humanity the value of suffering for the receipt of heavenly grace here on earth and to learn the lesson that this life is only temporal and we should embrace the heavenly course. For we are spiritual beings having an earthly experience. Ours is the recognition once enlightened to see that we are powerless over all things, the God of our own understanding has the power to grant or take away whatever he chooses for our spiritual, mental and bodily wellbeing. We are awakened too hand over to and be guided by our Higher Power.

Ours is the earthly lesson of giving in preference to taking. We are granted freewill to follow the way of God as co-creators in this time on earth or indeed reject Godly presence and lose the grace of falling to evil in all its forms. Our ego self prefers to do as it pleases as if it has the power of God and for a time seems allowed to follow such a course. Ultimately though we cannot close the door on our soul for our heart's love linked with God's ever forgiveness will prevail. We suffer much for our transgressions as equally as we suffer for God's grace. The suffering for God's grace however leads us to the light of salvation whereas the self ego suffering will lead only to desolation and death.

It is fitting that I address Buddha, the first of the Avatars of suffering and enlightenment, for he roamed the earth six centuries before Christianity, making his religious philosophy one of the oldest still being practised today.

Siddhartha Gautama, the founder of Buddhism, was born around 580 BC as a Prince of Sakya, a kingdom in the fertile plains at the foothills of the Himalayas. He was born into luxury and had every worldly pleasures at his disposal. During his youth he lived in three different palaces- one for the winter, one for the summer and one for the rainy season. His father kept him entertained with beautiful dancing girls and musicians, so that he would not be tempted to venture out into the world. Siddhartha enjoyed good health and was proficient at many sports, particularly archery. He lived that life of luxury and didn't leave his sumptuous palaces until age 29. He was always known to be very compassionate, even from his childhood. He had never known the realities of the world outside the walls of his confinement. When Siddhartha did finally venture out to see the world with his charioteer, he came upon firstly, a diseased man, then a senile old one, a corpse and a funeral ceremony with grieving relatives and finally a wandering holy man. On the fourth trip out of his confinement, he met up with the wandering holy man whose asceticism inspired him to follow a similar path in search of freedom from suffering that caused the endless cycle of birth, death, and rebirth. Upon witnessing the cycle of life for the first time, Siddhartha reportedly exclaimed: "This is the end which has been fixed for all, and yet the world forgets, it fears and takes no heed. Turn back the chariots, there is no time or place for pleasure excursions. How could an intelligent person pay no heed at a time of disasters, who knows of his impending destruction."

It is said that from there the Gods sent forth a religious mendicant who told Siddhartha that it was his mission to deliver mankind from suffering. " O, Bull among men,." the mendicant said: "I am a recluse who, terrified by birth and death, has adopted a homeless life to win salvation! Since I ask this way to live, my extinction is doomed, salvation from the world is what I wish and so I search for that most blessed state in which extinction is unknown." Reportedly, the mendicant then rose to the sky like a bird and vanished. It was upon this vision that Siddhartha intuitively perceived and made a plan to leave the palace as a homeless man. He renounced his rich upbringing and decided to become a monk. He had been instructed to marry at age 16, but left his wife of 13 years and their young son, and embarked upon a journey to seek the meaning of life. Wandering, he searched for Enlightenment, he studied and tried Hinduism and the Jain faith. The teachers were reported to have psychic powers, but the teachings did not satisfy him. He abandoned the teachings because the practice of the times followed sacrifices and rituals beyond the common man. So this is when he became ascetic. The Buddha looked inward to seek knowledge, then sought the advice of a holy man and for the next six years he became ascetic, attempting to conquer the innate appetite of food, sex and comforts by engaging in various yoga disciplines. Self punishment became a diet of pleasure in reverse, a kind of addiction, so he moved on. He soon realised that he was near death from fasting, So he accepted a bowl of rice from a young girl. After eating some more he regained his strength and realised physical austerity was not the way to spiritual liberation. "this is not the Dharma (cosmic law) leading to dispassionate life, to enlightenment, to emancipation. Inward calm cannot be maintained unless physical strength is constant, and intelligently replenished." It was how he gained spiritual strength to win enlightenment. His journey gave him the vision to fulfil his quest. In an earthly sense he pointed the way to enlightenment, but did not cross that bridge. Perhaps he would have if he had not taken the poisoned food that ended his earth life. Then again, he may have had the vision to see Christ's suffering as the catalyst to man's salvation and knew that it was not his spiritual mission to take that path.

For the last six months of his life The Buddha suffered greatly. Then in the agony of his being he saw the way to his spiritual realm. Whilst he suffered much in the physical sense, his soul and his spirit was in grace. He saw in his spirit the afterlife after so many of his inner journeys. The vision of being fed his last meal at the home of a poor man was a great honour to that man. Lord Buddha would be his guest, but he had nothing to feed him except mushrooms. This man was a farmer who grew mushrooms in wood in dirty places on rainy days. Due to the passing of a snake at the location, the mushrooms become poisonous but the poor farmer didn't know of this at the time. The snake had died at the very location of the newly acquired food, so the snake poison entered the mushrooms. The poor man had unknowingly made a poisonous vegetable soup for his dinner guest. When the Buddha ate he could taste the bitter poison, but so as not to offend his host ate the soup all the same.

It was not until after he left the man's home that he became gravely ill. The man himself tasted the soup and realised the error in feeding his Godly master and was greatly troubled. The Buddha realised he was dying and told a follower to explain to the poor man that the Buddha believed he was lucky to eat the soup and for him not to be troubled by it. The Buddha only smiled and it is reported that he stated: "This thunderbolt was bound to fall. What difference does it make which way I enter the kingdom? As far as I am concerned, no lightning has fallen on me because I have known who the nectar is. There is no death. Another will follow in many centuries to come who will be the light within the light. Look to him in your sadness, for in your days he is the way, the truth and the light in your journey inward."

Aeons before Christ was born to this earthly realm, Judaism, the faith of the holy fathers existed. In fact this religious belief dates back nearly 4000 years. Followers of Judaism believe in one God who revealed himself through the ancient prophets as depicted in the Bible. Traditionally, Judaism holds that Yahweh, the God of Abraham, Isaac and Jacob and the devine guardian of the Israelities, delivered them from slavery in Egypt, and gave them the Law of Moses at Mount Sinai, beginning with the Ten Commandments that God gave to the Israelites through Moses. It includes many rules of religious observance given in the first five books of the Old Testament (in Judaism these books are called the Torah). Jews traditionally believe God is only one, which is both wholly independent of, and removed from, the material universe) and involved in the material universe.

Jew's biblically believe God is conceived as unique and perfect, free from all faults, deficiencies, and defects, and further held to be Almighty, ever present, boundless and knowing everything, and complete in all of his attributes, who has no partner or equal, being the sole creator of everything in existence. In Judaism, God is never portrayed as an image. The Torah specifically forbade ascribing partners to share his singular sovereignty, as he is considered to be the absolute one without a second, indivisible, and incomparable being, who is similar to nothing and nothing is comparable to him. Thus, God is unlike anything in or of this world and is beyond all forms of human thought and expression. 'I am God, and there is none like me. Declaring the end from the beginning, and from ancient times the things that are not yet done saying, 'My counsel shall stand, and I will do all my pleasure:' (Isaiah 46: 10-1).

The Jewish race throughout history have suffered horrendously due in no small part to their Godly belief as many biblical stories detail. None are more telling than the holocaust realities of the 20th century. Of course, Jesus was a Jew. He was born of a Jewish mother, in Galilee, a Jewish part of the world. All of his friends, associates, colleagues, disciples, all of them were Jews. He regularly worshipped in Jewish communal worship, what we call synagogues. It seems by all biblical accounts that he brought the suffering upon himself by becoming a living sacrifice, dying by crucifixion to cleanse mankind of all wrongdoing in the eyes of God the Father. Jesus was only on earth as a man for a short time. As his story unfolds, He was visited by shepherds as a witness to his coming, for they had been already told by an angel of his birth. Likewise Magi Kings had followed a star from the east to the place of his birth, offering gifts of gold, frankincense and myrrh.

Apart from his preaching to the priests of the temple at age 12, he goes missing for 18 years and next appears when he returns from 40 day of fasting in the desert and is baptised by John the Baptist in the river Jordan. He preaches for the next three years to his followers, performs many miracles, predicted future events, and ultimately sacrificed himself on the cross for the wrongdoings of mankind, died and was buried at age 33, rose again from the dead three days later, visited his followers and ascended into the heavens. Jesus not only fulfilled his own spoken prophecy in his lifetime, he predicted events that were to come to pass some time in the future. One of the ministries was that of a prophet. Jesus had predicted that 'heaven and earth will pass away, but my words will not pass away' (Mathew 24:35)-to date his words still echo throughout Christendom, read and believed by untold millions.

Mary of Bethany poured oil on the body of Jesus in her anticipation of his death. She was rebuked by the disciples for wasting the oil. Jesus chastised them saying that her story would be retold wherever the gospel was preached. This has always come to pass. Jesus also predicted that one of his own would betray him. This was literally fulfilled by Judas. Jesus predicted that Peter would deny him three times before the cock crowed. This too came to pass. He predicted that he would suffer at the hands of religious rulers. On the night he was arrested the religious rulers allowed him to be beaten. Jesus predicted he would die in Jerusalem and upon a cross. Both predictions took place. He predicted that he would die during the Passover and would rise again in three days. This is well documented as having occurred as he predicted.

Many other events such as the destruction of the City of Jerusalem within one generation, the destruction of the Temple, the scattering of the Jewish people from their land, their captivity and the ruling of the Holy land by the Gentiles, the persecution of the Jewish people and though persecuted, the nation of Jews would survive. All of these predictions have been literally fulfilled. These facts demonstrate beyond any doubt that Jesus was indeed a genuine prophet. During his earthly ministry Jesus touched and transformed countless lives. Like other events in the life of Jesus, all his miracles were documented by eyewitnesses. The Gospels record 37 of these and are mentioned in various texts by the four writers Mathew, Mark, Luke and John. The ability at age 12 to interpret holy scriptures and teach wise scribes and priests in the Temple of Jerusalem would seem like a miracle to them at the time. But how he suffered so in his manhood for becoming a sacrificial lamb as an offering to God for the sins of mankind.

The most telling of the life of Jesus Christ on earth has been told and retold for over two thousands years. The story of Christ's last supper, agony in the garden of Gethsemane, his suffering on the way to Calvary, the crucifixion, resurrection and ascension into heaven, has been the basis of all Christian religious belief and reenactment ever-sense. The actions of the man of sorrows in his last 24 hours on earth is ingrained in the minds and hearts of every Christian who has ever lived. It was not so much how he died that we are mindful of but the reason he chose that way of suffering to cleanse the sin of man is what is so unique. Sure, the dying and rising of Jesus from the dead is consistent with the notion of divine individuals in pagan Gods, biblical reference- where the notion of regeneration is prevalent, Jesus' death and resurrection fits right in with these common and universal mythical belief patterns. Early educated Christians drew upon Jewish, Greek and later Roman sources in this regard. Christianity created a cache of Jesus sayings that contained historical and non-historical inspired sayings about the name of Jesus, his divinity and the realm of the Kingdom of God. Whilst commentary on the parables of his life and sayings is made up, the use of the parables as a moral or spiritual lesson is not.

The proof of the existence of Jesus's life, death and resurrection is well documented in history and the words of prophets, sages, philosophers and scribes as well as the oldest of all reference books, the Bible confirms this fact. The manifestation of his miracles and teachings are well documented. But it's not so much what he said or did during his life, but what he did at his end that is the crux of his story. For it's all about his suffering as a man and not so much that it was said of his being the son of God. Whilst he reportedly said: " I and the Father are one," (John 10:30) there is no biblical text or record in history of him saying that he was God. You get no argument from me of his existence be that the logical linear brain of belief or his rising from the dead. True or not, his time on earth, resurrection and ascension into the heavenly realm, Christ the Saviour is what still floats my boat. It is Christ in the manifested, the risen Lord that is my guiding light in this present hour. But I am getting away from the point. Of his last 24 hours, I wish to lay claim too. You may recall that in ancient Jewish custom it was traditional to make a sacrifice of a lamb at the temple altar, which was slaughtered, cooked and shared as a spiritual communion with the people. The smoke from this ritual cooking rising up to the heavens was viewed from outside a curtain enclosure by those presenting the offering to God who later shared by eating the flesh of the animal. A similar event took place with the poor who presented birds and other animals to participate in this Godly revenant proceeding. The night before he was put to death it may do well to reconsider what has been written of that night. Judas, may be construed as betraying Jesus in good faith to (perhaps) save him from being killed. For to hand him over to the Roman soldiers to be locked up until after Passover it would appear to have been a wise decision. For it was during a Sabbath day of the Passover that Jesus had made a spectacle in the presence of Roman soldiers, the scribes and priesthood and the multitude in attendance, by whipping merchants and traders at the entry of Temple gateway. He had reportedly stated "My house is a house of prayer, but you have made it a den of thieves." (Matthew 21:13, Luke 19:46)

Judas in his approach to the priests to arrange for Jesus's capture was paid thirty pieces of silver for it was customary to be paid for services rendered. It must be remembered that Jerusalem was an outpost of the Roman Empire at the time, and Pilot, the local Roman Governor, did not want any bad report of his management of the territory being sent back to Rome. He wanted to stay on side with the Jewish priesthood and endorsed any actions on their behalf to keep the peace. It is my opinion that Jesus, like many other rebellious leaders of the time, was considered a trouble maker. So when Jesus was ultimately handed over for questioning by the betrayal of Judas, the Roman governor, the priests and Judas were possibly relieved. But there is more to this story than meets the eye, so let's take a closer look at the character of Judas Iscariot and his betrayal of Jesus – for which, famously, he was paid thirty pieces of silver.

After the Last Supper, which will be discussed in a separate post here, Jesus retired with his disciples to the Garden of Gethsemane. In the Garden of Gethsemane, Judas Iscariot betrayed Jesus to the Romans by identifying him in public so they could seize Jesus and arrest him. Judas pointed out Jesus to the authorities by kissing him in greeting. Gethsemane was just outside the city of Jerusalem on the slopes of the Mount of Olives, which was far enough away from danger for Jesus in the view of his Apostles and no doubt would have been endorsed by Judas. Although Judas Iscariot was with them at the Last Supper, it is stated (or merely implied) in some Gospels that he left before the meal had ended. So he was not with Jesus and the other disciples when they went to Gethsemane. John (18:2) tells us that Jesus often went to this garden with his disciples, so Judas knew where to find Jesus. He told his disciples to sit while he went and prayed. There was clearly something on

Jesus' mind, as he took Peter and 'the two sons of Zebedee' with him to go and pray. Jesus fell on his face and prayed to God, asking to be relieved of the suffering to come. For it is biblically reported that he wept tears of blood. To my mind, he was an Avatar. He had the ability to see the past as well as the future and would have viewed the sin of mankind from the beginning of time and could foresee the sin of man to this very day after he suffered and died. Nevertheless, if it was God's will that it should be done, he was resigned to it. When he returned to Peter and the others, they'd fallen asleep, and he chastised them. Could they not watch with him, just for an hour? Jesus went and prayed three times in total, but each time, the disciples fell asleep. In the end, he told them to get some rest because the time had arrived for him to be betrayed by his enemies.

Shortly after this, Judas arrived with a crowd of priests carrying swords and sticks. Judas had arranged to reveal to them which man was Jesus by going up to Jesus and kissing him in greeting. When he did this, the crowd of priests knew which man to seize, so they grabbed Jesus and began to take him away. But Peter intervened, drawing his sword and lashing out at the servant of the high priest. His blade sliced off the man's ear, but Jesus commanded Peter to put his sword up, as he was prepared to do God's will and allow himself to be arrested. And Jesus reached out and healed the wounded man, restoring his ear. Judas' betrayal of Jesus is obviously a turning-point in the Gospels because it precipitates Jesus' arrest, interrogation, and subsequent crucifixion. But why Judas turned traitor is a difficult question to answer. Matthew (who is the Evangelist who wishes to match Jesus' life to Old Testament prophecies) is the only one of the four Gospel-writers who tells us how much Judas received for betraying Jesus. But why 'thirty pieces of silver'? If we go back to the Old Testament, we find in Zechariah 11:12-13 that Zechariah received thirty pieces of silver for his labour. He takes them and throws them 'to the potter,' supposedly because he's insulted by this amount of money, and the chief priests purchase a field with the silver.

So it seems that Matthew chose this rather modest sum – when the authorities would probably have paid Judas a far greater amount for him to betray Jesus – in order to fulfil another prophecy. Judas' motive may well have been mercenary though, because John 12:6 tells us that Judas was 'a thief.' Scholars cannot agree, by the way, on what the 'Iscariot' of 'Judas Iscariot' means. Probably the most widespread interpretation is that it means 'man from Kerioth,' which identifies Judas as a Judean rather than a Galilean (all of Jesus' other disciples were from Galilee), although in truth nobody is quite sure where Kerioth was. However, alternative theories have been put forward, including the idea that it's a miss-transcription of 'Sicariot,' meaning 'dagger man' or 'terrorist' –after a group of assassins, the Sicarii, who concealed daggers beneath their cloaks and carried out murders amongst crowds of people in an effort to resist Roman rule in the region. These terrorists were also known as the Zealots, and because of the ardour with which they opposed Roman occupation, the word zealot came to be applied to any fervent or fanatical supporter of a cause. Indeed, another Judas, Judas of Gamala (sometimes known as Judas of Galilee), had led a bloody but unsuccessful revolution against Rome.

Another question to which there is no definitive answer is: why did Judas betray Jesus in the first place? We can obviously plump for the mercenary motive – it was all about the money for Judas – but if we pause and marvel at how cheaply Judas allowed his treachery to be bought by the authorities, we may feel dissatisfied with such an answer. Still another possibility is that Judas believed Jesus was the Messiah–hence his following Jesus in the first place–but that he grew disillusioned with Jesus' refusal to launch a revolt against the Roman powers who governed Judea. (Here, the fact that Judas was supposedly a Judean where the other disciples were from Galilee adds credence to this theory.) In his endlessly informative analysis of the New Testament, Asimov's Guide to the Bible: The New Testament: 2002, Isaac Asimov points us to John's account of Judas' betrayal. In John chapter 12, Judas objects to a whole jar of expensive ointment over Jesus' head (in preparation for his coming death). Asimov interprets this act as a symbol of Jesus' anointing as king, but also his failure to act as Judas wishes him too. Jesus' 'turn the other cheek' philosophy, perhaps, doesn't sit well with the anti-Roman Judas. But this analysis of Judas' motives is only conjecture.

But how did Judas die? Most people will answer, 'The Bible tells us that Judas was overcome with remorse and hanged himself.' But this isn't so. Or, rather, it is and it isn't. Just as David both did and didn't kill Goliath, so Judas both did and didn't hang himself. In chapter 27 of Matthew, we are told that he took his own life, but a different account is given in Acts 1:17-20. There we are told that Judas, having purchased a field with his thirty pieces of silver, fell 'headlong' and 'burst asunder in the midst, and all his bowels gushed out.' A rather gruesome viewpoint. What ever the method or reasoning of Judas's betrayal, and his ultimate suicide, he no doubt would have been privy to Jesus's flogging by the Roman soldiers, the crowning of thorns embedded in his head, the carrying of his cross up the steep hill of Calvary and the nailing of his body at the crucifixion to his last breath. What more can one add of one man's sacrifice for mankind, and another's betrayal.

At the last supper, mindful of his pending death the next day, he gathered the disciples around him and whilst they were eating he broke the bread, gave it to them, and said, "Take, eat; for this is My body." And when He had taken a cup and given thanks, He gave it to them, saying, "Drink from it, all of you; for this is My blood of the covenant, which is poured out for many for forgiveness of sins. But I say to you, I will not drink this fruit of the vine from now on until that day when I drink it again with you in My Father's kingdom." After singing a hymn, they went out to the Mount of Olives. (Matthew 26:26-30). Here is where Christ turned the Jewish faith and ritual belief upside down. He had died so that we might be saved, the sacrificial lamb of God who relieves us of our inherent defects of character and by his act redeemed mankind with the 'grace of God.' Good karma prevailing for mankind, grace descending upon our soulful hearts and the free gift to call upon his Almighty Father, himself likewise as the son of God and foremost in our day as the third person of the 'Trinity of God,' if one seeks to believe that way, is always within our grasp if we meditate upon it. So practising mindfulness as Christ dictated in his Sermon on the Mount is to appreciate the need for his grace-that gift that can only be absorbed by doing unto others as they would have us do unto you. Those five adjectives of mercy, grace, faith, forgiveness and steadfastness seem to be the catalyst of human action for the betterment of oneself and our fellow man. If that's all there is to it, then it's worth a shot to try this Christ credo for a better life- being a believer or a non believer.

Next came the prophet Muhammad, of whom it is traditionally said was born in 570 in Mecca and to have died in 632 in Medina, where he had been forced to emigrate. Muslims believe that the Quran was orally revealed by God to this final prophet, Muhammad, through the archangel Gabriel incrementally over a period of some 23 years, beginning in the month of Ramadan, when Muhammad was 40; and concluding in 632, before the year of his death in 622. It is true that both Jesus and Muhammad, as well as all true prophets from Adam, Noah, etc. (peace be upon them all), carried essentially the same message: Islam, that is, monotheism and submission to the will and guidance of God. However, the details were not identical, but varied to cope with the time and nation addressed.

In Islamic interpretation, [Jesus (peace be upon him) was sent specifically to the Israelites, Muhammad (peace be upon him) was sent to all humanity. This was emphasised by Jesus as well: "But he answered and said, 'I am not sent but unto the lost sheep of the house of Israel.'] (Matthew 15:24). In contrast, the Qur'an declares the universal message of Islam. The Qur'an says what it means: {Say: "O people! surely I am the Messenger of Allah to you all, of Him whose is the kingdom of the heavens and the earth; there is no God but He; He brings to life and causes to die; therefore believe in Allah and His Messenger, the illiterate Prophet who believes in Allah and His words, and follow him so that you may walk in the right way."} (Al-A'raf 7:158)

So any distorted viewpoints of Islamic belief seem to contradict those of Christianity in interpretation. However, it is fair to say that some are spot on in the religious code of the Islamic sacred book, the Qur'an. A viewpoint here is a good example of the difference in Christian belief as to Islamic. [While Jesus's emphasis was on moral salvation and reform of the individual, with only a few rulings on marriage and divorce, etc., the final message of Islam brought a detailed comprehensive code dealing with all aspects of human life: personal, family, social, economic, political, and international. Jesus stressed purifying the soul; Muhammad was to build and maintain the model: individual, society, and nation.]

The Islamic sacred book, believed to be the word of God as dictated to Muhammad by the archangel Gabriel and written down in Arabic. The Koran consists of 114 units of varying lengths, known as *suras*; the first sura is said as part of the ritual prayer. These touch upon all aspects of human existence, including matters of doctrine, social organisation, and legislation. So it is that we get a different slant on the two prophets of God and their purpose for the faithful's belief. One form is of the Christian New Testament whilst the other is the Koran. So it is said by the Koran that it is true that both Jesus and Muhammad, as well as all true prophets from Adam, Noah, etc. (peace be upon them all), carried essentially the same message: Islam, that is, monotheism and submission to the will and guidance of God. (However, the details were not identical, but varied to cope with the time and nation addressed.). While Jesus (peace be upon him) was sent specifically to the Israelites, Muhammad (peace be upon him) was sent to all humanity. This was emphasised by Jesus as well: "But he answered and said, 'I am not sent but unto the lost sheep of the house of Israel.'" (Matthew 15:24)

In contrast, the Qur'an declares the universal message of Islam. The Qur'an says what it means: {Say: "O people! surely I am the Messenger of Allah to you all, of Him Whose is the kingdom of the heavens and the earth; there is no God but He; for He brings to life and causes to die; therefore believe in Allah and His messenger, the illiterate Prophet who believes in Allah and His words, and follow him so that you may walk in the right way."} (Al-A`raf 7:158) Blessed is He who sent down the criterion to His servant, that it may be an admonition to all creatures } (Al-Furqan 25:1) {And We have not sent you but to all the men as a bearer of good news and as a warner, but most men do not know.} (Saba' 34:28).

While Jesus's emphasis was on moral salvation and reform of the individual, with only a few rulings on marriage and divorce, etc., the final message of Islam brought a detailed comprehensive code dealing with all aspects of human life: personal, family, social, economic, political, and international. Jesus stressed purifying the soul; Muhammad was to build and maintain the model: individual, society, and nation. It is the viewpoint of Islamic belief that, during the seventh century CE when Muhammad (peace be upon him) was sent, there were only a few groups of followers of the original message and teachings of Jesus. The words we now know are New Testament interpretations by the Gospels of the Four Evangelists Matthew, Mark, Luke, and John, the authors attributed with the creation of the four canonical Gospel accounts. In the New Testament, they bear the following titles: the Gospel of Matthew; the Gospel of Mark; the Gospel of Luke; and the Gospel of John. According to those of islamic faith today the real word of Jesus no longer existed in any form, as was the case of the Torah of Moses before him. They were replaced according to Islamic scribes with the Old and New Testaments written by different human authors selected and sanctioned as holy by the Church ecumenical councils, several centuries after the departure of Jesus.

\It is their opinion, therefore, that it was high time then to re-establish the eternal guidance of the Creator to all humanity, but this time in a final eternal form, through the Glorious Qur'an and the detailed teachings and living model of the Prophet Muhammad (peace be upon him). Jesus prophesied the coming prophet whose universal message will stay forever is a total misrepresentation of the words of John the Baptist: "He is the one who comes after me, the thongs of whose sandals I am not worthy to untie." (John 1:27). For it was of Jesus that he spoke and not of Muhammad. And another: "And I will ask the Father, and he will give you another Counsellor to be with you forever—"(John 14:16). However, not to be too critical of others' belief, for good karma can always be emulated from the Quran for the benefit of any believer in a God of their own understanding. The Quran repeatedly reminds and draws attention to the Prophet Muhammad (peace be upon him) to his obligations towards Allah, the revelation, the believers, and the unbelievers.(Qur'an 75:16-18, 20:114, 87:6-7, 10:109 and 10:15-16.) He was also repeatedly exhorted and warned against yielding to the temptations and pressures that were surrounding him. (Qur'an: 17:73-75, 13:37-38, 5:49, 2:145, 2:120, 5:67, 6:14, 6:114, 11:112, 15:88, 68:48 and 72: 21-22.) In addition, the Qur'an included admonitions that were directed to the noble Prophet (peace be upon him) in some situations. (Qur'an: 4:105-109, 9:43, 9:117, 9:113, 6:52, 8:67-68, 66:1 and 80:1-11.)

Sometimes the Qur'an revealed matters that he would have preferred to keep secret in the depths of his pure soul. (Qur'an: 33:37.). It is difficult for a sound mind to imagine that the noble Prophet Muhammad (peace be upon him) would address himself with the aim of guidance, exhortation, warning, and admonishment, or would reveal things about himself that he would not like other people to know about. Also, it is difficult to believe that the Prophet Muhammad (peace be upon him) would, after doing that, convey to the people the Qur'an, which would never be abrogated, deleted, or forgotten. Occasionally, the revelation was delayed for weeks or months, despite the urgent need of the Prophet Muhammad (peace be upon him) to refute the hypocrites and the slanderers. Examples for this are the Qur'an verses 24:11-17 and 93:1-3. The Prophet even used his own discretion in interpreting some verses, until revelation was sent down contradicting his opinion. An example of this is verses 9:80-84.

The Prophet delivered the revealed message and fought for it, against all odds. His whole twenty-three years of prophethood were years of hardships The first thirteen years he and his followers were persecuted, tortured, and boycotted by the pagans of Makkah. He refused all offers of kingdom, wealth, or reconciling his message with their pagan beliefs. The following ten years, after immigration to Madinah, witnessed a harsh continuous struggle to spread the faith, with incessant fighting against the hostilities of Arab tribes and Madinah Jews, as well as the preludes to confrontation with the great Roman and Persian Empires. His personal life was the simplest and most ascetic of his contemporaries. Allah supported him and his few early followers with unexpected victories in spite of their poverty, physical weakness, and military and technical inexperience. His message was supported and spread to every corner of the world in a brief time. According to Islamic belief (no human being could have such a biography unless he is a true messenger of God, and truly he was. Allah rewards him for what he honestly delivered and for his striving for the salvation of all nations and generations.) Muhammad is not mentioned explicitly or; implicitly in the Bible, God's oldest written revelation (and the only written revelation as far as Christians are concerned). But Christ Jesus is found in the Quran. And what it says about Him places Him far above the founder of Islam.

There are so many stories told of suffering souls in the ancient history books other than those of the three Avatars in this chapter. None is more telling than the story of the sufferings of Job in the Bible. In the book of Job is a story that details the life of one man who was not a distinguished church figure facing persecution. He was an everyday man, albeit affluent in possessions and faith. The Bible describes Job's financial stature as making him a noteworthy person in his region of the east. He had a large family, a wife, seven sons, and three daughters. In his possession were also large quantities of land and animals (Job 1:2-3). Of all that he owned, his greatest asset was his faith. "There was a man in the land of Uz, whose name was Job; and that man was perfect and upright, and one that feared God, and eschewed evil." (Job 1:1) Job's ability to believe was so impressive that he garnered the attention of God and also Satan.

Satan confesses to roaming about the Earth, and God asks if the Devil has considered Job. The question sets Job up for an intense season of suffering, one that breaks him physically, emotionally, even spiritually, but he never forsakes his faith. All this occurs as a test, allowed by God to show Satan Job's faith (Job 1:11-12). Job's story continues to be relevant to Christians today because of his ability to believe despite suffering. His season of loss is a reminder that no possession or relation found himself losing all that he owned, all except for his faith. However, Job's story is not limited too suffering or maintaining faith amid trials. There are a number of different lessons we can glean, but first, we must understand the purpose of the Book of Job and why it was included in the Bible. Job did not commit any sin that led to his suffering. On the contrary, Job's suffering came about as God allowed Satan to test his faith. Why did Job have to suffer at all?

The same question has been asked throughout the ages after events such as school shootings or natural disasters. Why do innocent people suffer for seemingly no reason? And Job was so greatly afflicted by his problems that he cursed, not God, but the day that he was born. "After this, Job began to speak and cursed the day he was born." (Job 3:1) This was not an inconvenience that Job experienced. Life as he knew it was turned upside down and made into something that brought him intense pain. Job represents the truth that innocent people suffer, but by the end of his story also shows that God is in control the entire time. God allowed Satan to attack Job spiritually, emotionally, and physically, but never to the point of death (Job 2:6). God remained in control. As shown in the Psalms, which follow after the Book of Job, prayer is shown to be communication with God that is deep, intimate, and honest. "If I have sinned, what have I done to you, Watcher of humanity? Why have you made me your target, so that I have become a burden to you?"(Job 7:20)

In his anguish and confusion, Job sought to have dialogue with God as a means of understanding his plight. We are like Job when we experience suffering. We may ask God questions like "How long?" or "Why is this happening to me?" Though not immediately, God does respond to Job later in the book (Job 38). God also answers our prayers, just in His own timing. In the way God responds to Job, He makes clear that though we may ask, our sense of comprehension will never fully grasp God and His ways. Still, He is trustworthy. Job's loved ones didn't help because Job's wife was the first to reveal her lack of faith in God. "His wife said to him, 'Are you still holding on to your integrity? Curse God and die!'" (Job 2-9)

Job's response shows just how much faith he had in spite of her doubts. "You speak as a foolish woman speaks,' he told her. 'Should we accept only good from God and not adversity?' Throughout all this Job did not sin in what he said" (Job 2:10). Job proposed an excellent question to consider. If God promises salvation in the form of heaven, why is life expected by some to only be good? Job's three friends when introduced to the story bear witness to his suffering. They go so far as to lament on his behalf (Job 2:13). As the Book of Job continues each friend has a chapter where they engage in dialogue with Job. Then Job is given a chapter where he responds. The friends' attempts to "help" go so poorly that God is ultimately disappointed in them (Job 42:7). God was so upset he had them offer sacrifices as repentance.

The reason for this is that the friends blamed Job for his suffering, unbeknownst to them God allowed Job to suffer despite being a righteous man. His friend Eliphaz was the first to blame Job. "Consider: Who has perished when he was innocent" (Job 4:7)? Their relationship helps us see how we as believers seek counsel from others. While people may mean well in their advice-giving, no one can truly comprehend how God works in our lives and should not speak on His behalf. Moreover, suffering is to be experienced even by the innocents, like Job, not because someone has committed an offence against God, but because suffering is a part of life. God used Job's suffering to build him up and show the Devil that Job would keep his faith. Job Was Restored: "After Job had prayed for his friends, the Lord restored his fortunes and doubled his previous possessions." (Job 42:10)

In the end, Job gained more than he lost. And he was restored in all aspects of his life: health, family, finances. God showed Job favour as he remained faithful in his belief. This information is important because these details reflect the loving nature of God. God's love was present despite Job's unhelpful friends, wife, and harsh circumstances. God does not allow sorrow for the sake of suffering. He allows us to experience trials to make us better people and expose weak areas in our lives. Job was able to learn more about God during his struggle and further build his trust in the Lord.

Job's suffering too also allowed God to affect Job's friends. They initially blamed Job and learned that Job hadn't done anything to merit his suffering, thus, showing them a side of God they were unaware of before. Job Kept His Faith.

Throughout the entire book, Job prayed, struggled, and eventually overcame. He never stopped having a relationship with God. Nor did he curse God as his wife encouraged him to do in the second chapter. Job's steadfast faith offers proof that no matter life's circumstances, maintaining faith is always a possibility. Whether we are spiritually, emotionally, or physically stricken, we can keep our trust in God. He will at some point deliver us from our troubles, and make us better from the experience. As we read and learn from Job we can ascertain that suffering comes upon all, sinful or guiltless. Jesus was the only person without sin and even He knew suffering. While we may encounter our own unexpected problems like Job, his story reminds us that even when we don't understand why we can put trust in God. That trust is not limited to circumstances, nor by the "advice" given by other believers. Trust is not an explanation of why Job suffered, or why we suffer. Yet, the idea of trust gives us a solution to bear the suffering. No one can fully understand God, and that gives us all the more reason to pray. And when we pray and while we wait, we know in the end God will make us into someone better than where we started. Job proved that.

One bread, One body, One Lord of all,
One cup of blessing which he blessed,
And we though many throughout the earth,
We are one body in this one Lord.

Gentile or Jew, Servant or free,
Women or men, no more.

One bread, One body, One Lord of all,
We are one body in this one Lord.

CHAPTER 5.

LEGENDS ON FOOT

The following content in this chapter is about the lives of people whose certain personal sacrifice have made them living legends, in my lifetime. I write in brief of their trials and tribulations, sufferings and commitment to their chosen fields for the benefit of others and ultimately their own inner harmony.

Mohanadas Karamchand Gandhi was born in 1869 into a wealthy political family. His father Karamchand Gandhi was the chief minister for the princely state of Gujarat, western India, and taught him the political astuteness that served him so well later in life. His mother taught him the tenets of her faith in the Jain religion; the sanctity of life, vegetarianism, abstinence from alcohol, fasting for self purification, and mutual tolerance across all creeds and sects. These principles helped to frame and guide his adult life. Age 19, in 1888 he went to University College in London to study law. There as a practising Jain, he joined the Vegetarian Society, was elected to the executive committee, and founded a local chapter. He later credited this experience in shaping lessons in organisational behaviour.

Gandhi returned to India after being successfully admitted to the bar, to set up a law practice in Bombay. He ultimately ended up in his home town of Rajkot making a modest living drafting petitions for litigants. This ultimately failed due to the hostility of a local British officer. Frustrated and dispirited, in 1893 Gandhi accepted a year-long contract from an Indian legal firm in Natal, South Africa. It proved to be the makings of Gandhi, and the experience opened his eyes to dramatic forms of racial discrimination that were then evident. He was thrown out of court in Durban for refusing to remove his turban; he was **ejected from a train** at Pietermaritzburg after refusing to move from the first class coach to third class one, to make way for a white passenger; he was savagely beaten by a stagecoach driver for refusing to travel on the footboard to make room for a European passenger. Such incidents stirred Gandhi to the realisation of the racism and social injustice endemic in South Africa. On the termination of his year-long contract, Gandhi was persuaded to stay in South Africa to lead the legal fight against the National Legislative Assembly's proposed bill to deny Indians the right to vote. Although unable to halt the bill's passage, his campaign was successful in drawing attention to the grievances of the Indians of South Africa, and helped to found the Natal Indian Congress in 1894, with him as the secretary.

In 1896 Gandhi returned to India in order to bring his wife and children back to South Africa. On his return in January 1897, he was attacked by a white mob, who tried to lynch him. He refused to press charges against any of the mob, stating that it was one of his principles not to seek redress for personal wrongs in a court of law. It was an early indication of the values that would shape his later campaign against injustices. As the Second Anglo-Boer War got underway in 1899 Gandhi argued that Indians should support the British war effort against the Afrikaners in order to legitimise their claims to full citizenship. Accordingly, he organised a volunteer ambulance corps of 300 Indians and 800 indentured labourers, which became one of the few medical units prepared to serve wounded Black Africans. Gandhi himself acted as a stretcher bearer at the battle of Spion Kop, one of the many early disasters of the British forces-and he was subsequently decorated for it. After the war, however, there was still much to do. So in 1906 Gandhi announced a non-violent campaign against the Transvaal regional government's proposal to enforce registration of all Indians. Over the next eight years, thousands of Indians in South Africa were jailed, including himself and on many occasions, flogged, or even shot. They responded by striking, refusing to register, burning their registration cards and other forms of non-violent resistance.

Gandhi returned to India in 1914, joining the Indian National Congress the principal political grouping in the struggle against British rule for Indian self government. Here he initiated protests against social injustice. His first public success was won in 1918, in a campaign targeting Gujarati landlords, and their British protectors, who forced their tenants to grow indigo and other cash crops instead of the foodstuffs necessary for their survival. Gandhi organised a detailed study and survey of these villages, describing the atrocities and terrible episodes of suffering, and began a clean-up of the worst areas, building schools and hospitals. Unsurprisingly, he was soon arrested and ordered to leave the province, but hundreds of thousands of people protested outside the jails, police stations and courts demanding his release. Ultimately, the provincial government, prodded by the British, acceded to his demand, and it agreed to give the villagers control over their farming and compensation for their losses. By the end of the campaign Gandhi was being addressed as the 'Bapu' (Father) and 'Mahatma' (Great Soul) and his fame was spreading nationally.

In April 1919 General Reginald Dyer ordered his troops to open fire on an unarmed religious celebration in Amritsar, in the Sikh province of Punjab. Objection to British rule was running high and there was some disturbance. While the official report declared that 379 Indians had been killed, the probable death toll was more like 1000. In the aftermath of the massacre, leading politicians in Britain condemned the atrocity, and Indians rioted in the streets. Gandhi was careful not to criticise both Dyer and the retaliatory violence. He offered condolences to British civilian victims of the uprising and condemned the riots, to the rage of many within the Congress Party. However, by then Gandhi had come to the conclusion that Indian independence was the only way forward. So from December 1921 he helped reorganise the party with this one goal firmly in mind. Meanwhile Gandhi expanded his non-violent protest to include a boycott of foreign made goods, particularly British.

He advocated for homespun cloth to be the only fabric worn by Indians, and not British made textiles; if feasible, this cloth should be spun at home. At the same time, Gandhi exhorted Indian women to boycott British educational institutions and courts, to resign from government employment and to forsake British titles and honours. Gandhi's policy of non-cooperation enjoyed widespread success. However, violence erupted in Pradesh in February 1922 and Gandhi was encouraged to call off the campaign of mass civil disobedience. Two weeks later he was arrested, tried for sedition, and sentenced to six years in prison. He was incarcerated until February 1924, when he was freed after an operation for appendicitis.

Meanwhile, The Congress Party had begun to show signs of a split along religious fault lines between Hindus and Muslims. By December 1928 Gandhi was calling on the British government to grant India dominion status immediately, or face a new campaign of non-violence aimed at achieving complete independence. The British did not respond and on the 31st December1929 Gandhi launched a new campaign against the notoriously iniquitous tax on salt. There he published his intention for the famous 'Salt March' march to the sea at Dandy, where he proceeded to make salt himself. Thousands of Indians joined him in the march, and the subsequent result in the imprisonment of over 60,000 people. India's new Viceroy, Lord Irwin, later Earl of Halifax, opted to negotiate with Gandhi, and in March 1931 agreed to free all political prisoners. In return Gandhi agreed to call off the campaign at the Round Table Conference in London. The conference was a disappointment and on his return to India Gandhi was arrested yet again. In his civil disobedience and to represent the Indian National Congress protest, Gandhi embarked upon a six day fast in September 1932 and then a 21 day fast of self purification in May 1933.

When war broke out in 1939 Gandhi initially backed Britain, but other Congress leaders were offended by the Viceroy's unilateral declaration of the war on India's behalf. Gandhi eventually came to the conclusion that it would be nonsensical to support the war when India did not have democracy itself. Momentously, he launched a campaign demanding the British 'Quit India.' This resulted in the arrest of the entire Congress Working Committee in Bombay by the British authorities in August 1942. Gandhi was held captive for two years during which time his wife and personal secretary died.

Gandhi was released in May 1944 because of failing health. The following year in Britain, Clement Attlee's Labour government gave a clear indication that it was prepared to grant India independence, and Gandhi called the struggle off, encouraging the new Viceroyal, Lord Wavell, to release over 100,000 political prisoners. In the subsequent negotiations Gandhi was vehemently opposed to the partition of splitting up India along religious lines. However, Congress overruled him and approved the partition of the subcontinent into India and Pakistan as the only way to prevent a civil war between Hindus and Muslims. On the day of independence Gandhi did not celebrate with the rest of India. Instead, he was alone in Calcutta, mourning Partition and working to end the appalling outbreak of violence that accompanied it. He launched his last 'fast-for- hunger' in Delhi, asking that all communal violence be ended for all.

In such an eventful life Gandhi made enemies among fellow Indians, especially amongst those who hated his ecumenical respect for Muslims and Hindus alike. There were many attempts on his life at the time. On January 30th 1948 Gandhi was staying at a wealthy Birla family home in New Delhi. Here, the man described by India's Prime Minister Nehru as 'The Father of the Nation', finally fell victim to the kind of violence he had spent his life eschewing. Nathuram Godse, a Hindu radical who regarded Gandhi as an appeaser of Muslim Pakistan, shot and killed ' Bapu' as he was on his way to a prayer meeting. Gandhi's burial ceremony took place in New Delhi. The majority of his ashes were divided among all the major rivers of the world, from the Nile to the Thames, with a small portion being enshrined at the Mahatma Gandhi World Peace Memorial, within a thousand-year-old stone sarcophagus sent from China.

The man who suffered so much and sacrificed himself for the betterment of his country and humanity at large will always be remembered for his generosity of spirit, his humbleness, consideration for the welfare of his fellow man and placid demure irrespective of the difficult circumstances that surrounded him for the majority of his adult life.

Perhaps his most famous quote sums up the way of Gandhi's life the best: "Be that change that you wish to see in the world." And: "An ounce of patience is worth more than a tonne of preaching." "In a gentle way, you can shake the world." "The greatness of a nation and its moral progress can be judged by the way its animals are treated." He walked many a mile in pilgrimages with his walking staff for support and the some old well worn sandals on his feet in his mission of peace, harmony and goodwill for all.

Mother Teresa of Calcutta, was born Agnes Gonxha Bojaxhiu, and was baptised on August 27, 1910, in Skopje Macedonia in Republic of North Macedonia. The daughter of an ethnic Albanian grocer, she went to Ireland in 1928 to join the Sisters of Loretto at the Institute of the Blessed Virgin Mary and sailed only six weeks later to India as a teacher. She taught for 17 years at the Order's school in Calcutta. In 1946 Sister Teresa experienced her "call within a call," which she considered divine inspiration to devote herself to caring for the sick and poor. She then moved into the slums she had observed while teaching. Municipal authorities, upon her petition, gave her a pilgrim hostel, near the sacred temple of Kali, where she founded her Order in 1948. Sympathetic companions soon flocked to her aid. Dispensaries and outdoor schools were organised. Mother Teresa adopted Indian citizenship, and her Indian nuns all donned the sari as their habit. In 1950 her Order received canonical rites of the Roman Catholic sanction from Pope Pius XIII and in 1965 it became a pontifical congregation (subject only to the Pope). In 1952 she established Nirmal Hriday ("Place for the Pure of Heart "), a home where the terminally ill could die with dignity. Her Order also opened numerous centres serving the blind, the aged, and the disabled. Under Mother Teresa's guidance, the Missionaries of Charity built a leper colony, called Shanti Nagar ("Town of Peace "), near Asansol, India.

In 1962 the Indian government awarded Mother Teresa the Padma Shri, one of its highest civilian honours, for her services to the people of India. Pope Paul V on his trip to India in 1964 gave her his ceremonial limousine, which she immediately raffled to help finance her leper colony. She was summoned to Rome in 1968 to found a home there, staffed primarily with Indian nuns. In recognition of her apostolate, she was honoured on January 6, 1971, by Pope Paul, who awarded her the first Pope John XXIII Peace Prize. In 1979 she received the Nobel Peace Prize for her humanitarian work, and the following year the Indian government granted her the Bharat Ratna, the country's highest civilian honour.

In her later years Mother Teresa spoke out against divorce, abortion and contraception. She also suffered ill health and had a heart attack in 1989. In 1990 she resigned as Head of the Order but was returned to office by a nearly unanimous vote—the lone dissenting voice was her own. A worsening heart condition forced her retirement, and the Order chose the Indian-born Sister Nirmala as her successor in 1997. At the time of Mother Teresa's death, her Order included hundreds of centres in more than 90 countries with some 4,000 nuns and hundreds of thousands of lay workers. Within two years of her death, the process to declare her a saint was begun, and Pope John Paul 11 issued a special dispensation to expedite the process of canonization. She was beatified on October 19, 2003, reaching the ranks of the blessed in what was then the shortest time in the history of the Church. She was canonised by Pope Francis 1 on September 4, 2016.

Although Mother Teresa displayed cheerfulness and a deep commitment to God in her daily work, her letters (which were collected and published in 2007) indicate that she did not feel God's presence in her soul during the last 50 years of her life. The letters reveal the suffering she endured and her feeling that Jesus had abandoned her at the start of her mission. Continuing to experience a spiritual darkness, she came to believe that she was sharing in Christ's Passion, particularly the moment in which Christ asks, "My God, my God, why have you forsaken me?" Despite this hardship, Mother Teresa integrated the feeling of absence into her daily religious life and remained committed to her faith and her work for Christ. She died on September 5, 1997, in Calcutta, now Kolkata, India, the founder of the Order of the Missionaries of Charity, a congregation of women dedicated to the poor, particularly to the destitute of India.

Mother Teresa in her life's work left happiness to find joy. The difference between happiness and joy is that happiness avoids suffering and joy endures suffering in hope. To say that Mother Teresa left happiness to find joy means that she went towards suffering in hope. She once said: "I have found the paradox, that if you love until it hurts, there can be no more hurt, only more love. If you are humble nothing will touch you, neither praise nor disgrace, because you know what you are. Another of her quotes was, "If you judge people, you have no time to love them." "Peace begins with a smile." "We fear the future because we are wasting today."

Perhaps mindful of her pending death she stated: "If I ever become a Saint–I will surely be one of darkness." "I will continually be absent from Heaven–to light the light of those in darkness on earth," she said. "I do not pray for success, I ask for faithfulness. It's not how much we give but how much love we put into giving. We want to create hope for the person ... we must give hope, always hope." "Let no one ever come to you without leaving better and happier."

I was thinking of a dream I had back one night on my first Camino pilgrimage. It was about drinking to excess. It was in sharp contrast with the dream of the previous night- that of a beautiful maiden. I thought it strange my dream had not been of a Sword of Discernment, as my dreams on The Camino often were. Perhaps it was because I was sleeping in a monastery, or because of the influence of the Pilgrim's Prayer at the tomb of St. Juan de Ortega in the adjacent chapel. Then why the fair maiden and the drinking dreams?

I never did get a proper night's sleep on The Camino. If it was not someone talking in their sleep, snoring or farting in their sleeping-bag, it was the Italian bike riders flashing lights and whispering in the dark, quite oblivious to the sleeping throng in their nearby beds. The village of Ages was only about 3 km from the monastery, and it was far too early to have breakfast; the next village after Ages was 8 km further on, so I decided that would be a good goal to aim for to partake of my usual ritual breakfast. I quickly dressed, being careful not to make a noise, as things were now quiet after the Italians' departure. Once my eyes adjusted to the dark outside, I could make out the shadowed silhouette of the chapel behind me, and readied my walking poles for the task ahead. It had not occurred to me, the evening prior, to check for the Camino shell or yellow-arrowed directions to determine which way to take in the darkness. I realised that my headlamp and small hand torch were in the middle of my backpack and would be difficult to find in the darkness.

I stood for a moment to consider my options, whether to go back to bed until there was enough light to see by or to find the light in the monastery's registry office and find my headlamp and torch - or maybe just to hand over to whoever is running this show. My dilemma was solved in an instant when, out of the darkness, a white robe appeared like a ghost in the night. It was the monk I always saw kneeling in prayer whenever I entered a chapel or church. The fact that his daily journeys began when the majority of pilgrims were either still asleep or contemplating the coming day in the comfort of their beds was also the reason he was always ahead of me, even on days when I walked fast. He quickly moved along the track ahead of me and appeared to know the exact way to traverse the darkness.

The white robe was a beacon of light for me, so I quickly followed in his footsteps. Although I could now see the pathway beneath my feet, the monk's robe gave me added assurance. I wasn't sure for how long I could keep-up with his pace, as he was so athletic and moved very quickly in the dark. I had not followed him for more than five minutes when he suddenly took a left turn onto another track; I followed in haste as he quickened his pace. No more than one hundred metres along the path he suddenly stopped, about ten metres in front of me. I, too, stopped and waited for his next move as he raised his habit, turned his head towards me while facing his body away, and said, in English but with a Hungarian accent, "I am just taking a piss."

He identified himself as Brother John of the Order of Mother Theresa. This was his sixth Camino, and he did it in the manner of the early Camino de Santiago pilgrims. He had completed each previous Camino without carrying any food, water or money. He apparently asked for food from fellow pilgrims, who shared with him during the day – a custom of The Camino. In the evening, he approached restaurant owners for food. Sometimes they refused, but he overcame this by waiting until the owner had left the kitchen and returned to approach the cook, who, in the absence of the owner, gladly gave him food. Being The Camino, sharing both food and clothing is commonplace among pilgrims, and water is never an issue as it's always in plentiful supply at the villages' central-square fountains.

There's a story that the Christ's man told
of a pilgrim on his way,
from Jerusalem to Jericho
on that fate-filled day.

Fortune wasn't smiling
when he came across some thieves;
They robbed him and they stabbed him
left him there to bleed.

Now it happened that along that road
a priest was passing near;
he saw the young man lying there
but he passed him by.

Then came lawyer of business mind
who had more than he could spend;
he likewise ignored the man
and on the road he went.

Then came a man both strong and kind
who put him on his back,
carried him to a nearby inn
just a little way down the track.

He shared with him some of his food,
left money for his keep
and told the hotel owner
get him well, I'll pay upkeep.

The man we call a Samaritan,
it's the name of those of kind,
who put others before themselves,
help the poor, the drunk, the blind.

Now youth today walk on The Way
to discover their own soul,
whilst those of us towards our end,
we're letting-go of our load.

Santiago travellers,
doing their own thing,
They live on love for fellow man
determined to be free.

Boots.

You are my soul companion
as we walk The Camino Way,
faithful from morning to nightfall
tramping in step with me.

You're just an old pair of boots
worn weary, just like me
greeting my toe, feet and blisters
as we start the day.

Yesterday you were there for me,
today is the same on The Way;
in the evening we part company,
Tomorrow you will be here. I pray.

CHAPTER 6

YOGA & MEDITATION PRACTICE

Yoga's origins can be traced to northern India over 5000 years ago. The word yoga is mentioned in sacred text as 'Rig Veda.' The vedas are a set of four ancient sacred texts written in Sanskrit. The Rig Verda is the earliest amongst the vedas and is a collection of over 1000 hymns and mantras in ten chapters known as mandalas, which were used by the Vedic age priests. Yoga was refined and developed by sages who documented the practices and benefits in the Upanishads, a huge work containing over 200 scriptures. Yoga is amongst the six schools of philosophy in Hinduism, and also is a major part of Buddhism and its meditation practices. Yoga practice has traditionally focused on breathing, flexibility and strength to boost mental and general wellbeing.

The main components of yoga are breathing and postures; a series of breath and body movements designed to increase strength and flexibility. So getting the breathing right is pre-essential to the practice. We shall come back to the breathing, but first a little about the various postures. When starting yoga, there are certain postures which became the foundation of yoga practice. Anchoring the practice with these postures allows you to reap the benefits of yoga-flexibility, improving muscle strength, protection of the spine, increased blood flow, and even improved happiness.

It is essential to listen to the body with every posture taken in yoga. This can only be done correctly with the breath. The term 'Pranayama,' coming from ancient Sanskrit text, refers to the life force within every being. It is used to describe breathing exercise, which clears the physical and emotional obstacles in our body to free the breath. 'Ujjayi,' another ancient term, is translated as " Victorious breath." Ujjayi breath is performed by restricting the airflow at the back of the throat, while , often compared with the sound of the oceans. Modern Yoga teachers keep in mind the lifestyle needs in our current time and adapt the ancient practices into five main basic proper principles of **exercise, breathing, relaxation, diet, and meditation.**

All I will endeavour to do here is to give you the reader a little insight into the practice of yoga so that you can determine for yourself the benefits of learning this ancient craft. We shall take a brief look at each basic principle and you can then determine for yourself if you wish to join a Yoga class or not. I can only relate as a learner of the benefits to me despite the fact that I have but entered the doorway to this new realm of yoga over a ten year practice cycle. I still consider myself a novice and on a steep learning curve, and that is why I am skimming across the surface of this new way of life that you may feel like joining if you will. I am not a yoga teacher but can just relate what I am learning and practising.

It is nearly a decade ago that I was in my worst state of being on this planet. I was depressed and lost to the reality of life around me. Even more so I seemed to be void of feeling anything other than the discomfort of physical pain and mental torment. The spiritual realm of living in the light for me didn't exist back then. For me life was just a sense of total exhaustion, mental confusion and darkness. Fortunately I recovered to a new motivation for living in the light of day and a belief in a Higher power, a God of my own understanding. I also found the practice of yoga which has improved my mental wellbeing, physical posture and is a guiding light to my inner spirituality. Now, I have reached a point of practice where I am just beginning to get it.

Lets see what the experts say who have practised yoga over many lifetimes. [Yoga is—and always has been—first and foremost a spiritual discipline. And it's much more than physical postures; it's a comprehensive system for allying self-effort with divine grace in order to experience the eternal oneness of soul and spirit. Many people come to Yoga practice for physical therapy, or stress reduction, or most commonly, a fitness regime. Increasingly, those needs are being met by specialised approaches that, although they offer many benefits, often omit the spiritual dimension of Yoga. Now, with spiritual hunger growing worldwide, more and more people are asking, "How can Yoga help meet my spiritual needs?" They suspect that spiritual experience can be cultivated through Yoga practices—and they're right. More than just physical, it shows how to quicken spiritual growth by skilfully integrating the postures, breathing exercises, and of course meditation practice. In fact, any approach to Yoga can uplift your state of mind to some degree. It will uplift you even more if you practise with the right attitude, the most powerful spiritual tool of all. And still more is possible if you also co-operate actively with the inner workings of subtle energy and consciousness.}

This is excerpted from Nayaswami Spiritual Yoga in a quest to know a greater reality—beyond the senses, intellect, and emotions.

[Your concept of that reality might be cosmic: Spirit, Higher Power, Truth, God, Divine Mother. Or it might be very personal: soul, Higher Self, your own highest potential. Or it might be something else altogether. Yet for every spiritual seeker, the goal is the same: to experience that greater reality. Belief can't take us there. Although belief can motivate us and guide our efforts, it is not knowledge—and if we cling dogmatically to belief, it can keep us from knowing. Experience is the only source of knowledge.]

In Gyandev's book, Spiritual Yoga: Awakening to Higher Awareness, Paramhansa Yogananda put it simply: "The yogi must turn his conceptions into perceptions." Another great yogi, Swami Vivekananda, said, "It is no doubt a blessing to be born into a religion, but it is a misfortune to die in one." Both were urging people to go beyond belief and religion into direct, personal experience. Whilst there is some truth in that statement it is not entirely true, for spirituality through religious belief can be attained through meditative practice combined with yoga postures. It is not my place to dwell too much on another's belief or experience in this regard. It is just fine for me at least that the symbolism and signs of religious practice keep me on track on my inner journey. Like, saying a spiritual mantra or praying a Biblical Psalm, I find it far more uplifting and it helps towards my oasis of serenity in a busy head before I commence my yoga practice.

Of course I am a novice when it comes to inner harmony, but I am surely on a learning curve. In truth it is difficult to escape the regimentation and ingrained indoctrination of a black and white religious upbringing. It was only when my life fell apart that I found the old ways of belief no longer worked for me. So I left traditional religious practice altogether some two decades ago in the midst of many tragic circumstances that surrounded me. Religion didn't help, but spiritual manta practice and yoga did. Over time I gave it all away and turned to wandering the world in search of meaning and to recover from mental illness due to anxiety and stress. On my return home I found some solace in creative outlets, writing books and songs and marketing my work, but it didn't give me the peace and harmony I had been seeking. A realisation that the scaffolding of my old belief was drawing me back to the faith of my father's holy faith. I sometimes return to that belief. However, It is not the same approach to my spiritual way of life now. More like a meditative practice entering a church, taking in the symbolism of my old belief and using it to improve my inner spirit. My faith in Higher Power is more in the manifest than in my logical brain, and it seems to float my spiritual boat so to speak.

Now with yoga I am slowly learning to listen to my body, to the instructions of the yoga teacher with an inner ear. It is no longer a physical exercise for me although it does help in that regard. Yoga is for me a practice of being in tune with my body. The spiritual practice of listening to a preacher is altogether a different thing. The yoga teacher helps me attune to every aspect of each practice with clear concentration for the benefit of body, mind and spirit. The preacher gives guidance on biblical text from the new and old testaments which helps me live a truth according to the healing power of God for not just the benefit of myself but for that of my fellow man. I am not being saintly here, it is just how it is for me now, and maybe by stating it here, you the reader may gain some benefit and encouragement to turn to religious and yoga practice that best suits you.

Firstly, a couple of examples of Proper Exercise practice in Yoga. A good example here is a typical yoga practice. Stand very erect, with your chest open. Reach your arms overhead, bringing your body into the shape of the letter "Y." Gaze upward. Reach your entire body upward in the direction of your gaze. Inhale smoothly and deeply, hold your breath, and smile broadly. Stay in this position for a few moments, then exhale with a hearty laugh and relax your arms back down into a normal upright standing position. Breathe naturally. It is a typical beginning exercise for a yoga session. I will leave it to you to determine suitable yoga classes to attend depending upon your bent for a yoga practice.

Another simple practice is to sit cross legged in a yoga position. (Any yoga teacher will show you how to do this correctly). The idea is to sit upright in this position to ensure you're sitting on the tail bones of your buttock. Now focus with eyes closed in that position and gently rock forward and back 'feeling' the tail bones you are seated on and not the flesh part of the buttocks. It takes time to listen to the body in movement and do the practice. As to beneficial personal practices in yoga exercise there are a plethora of them. From standing postures, to sitting ones, those lying on your back to those lying on your stomach. Side postures, too forward and back ones and for the advanced students, those standing on your head.

I can but encourage you to yoga, for just as we lose our physical flexibility and strength when we have not been stretching our muscles regularly, we lose our emotional and cognitive flexibility and strength when we have not been "tested" or stepped out of those comfort zones.

If we aren't mindfully practising refraining, patience, non-reactivity, and compassion, as we do in yoga, we risk being "out of practice" and lacking such skills when tested. If yoga is the primary place we choose to do this, a hiatus from practice might not just affect your physical flexibility and strength–we also might lose our focus, or our calm, or our compassion. Fortunately, once learned, we are able to access these skills more quickly than we would have before learning them (think muscle-memory), as we've created the neural pathways; we just need to strengthen them ("neurone that fire together wire together"). Yoga offers many techniques that use the body to lift energy more powerfully than this—and the more energy you lift, the more you'll raise your consciousness.

Mantras have a role in the practice of yoga. Mantras are repetitive sounds used to penetrate the depth of the unconscious mind and adjust the vibration of all aspects of your being. Mantra can be chanted aloud, delved upon or listened into. In yoga, a manta in Sanskrit, is derived from the root of "man," meaning "to think," and "tra" meaning "to protect or free from bondage" or " free the mind." On a more sophisticated level mantras and melodies are phrases with spiritual interpretations. These can be many things, such as human longing for truth, reality, light, immortality, peace, or love. Some mantras have no literal meaning, but are meaningful from a spiritual standpoint.

Long before I ever considered yoga practice, I was drawn to mantra practices which lead to meditation and ultimately yoga. At my worst state of being I was an emotional, physical and spiritual wreck. Back in 2002 it all came to a head after ten major personal catastrophic events came down upon me. The break up of a long standing marriage, the loss of home and family unity, the scattering of my children far and wide, consequences of loss of material possessions in the divorce, the court case that followed, the loss of business, the flood of devastation of the suicide of a friend, the accidental death of another, the deterioration of my mother's health, the rape of a blood relative and the straw that broke the camels back; the suicide of my second eldest son. All these events transpired over a two year timeframe. I began to drink heavily unaware then that I was already a full blown alcoholic. I could not sleep and ultimately I collapsed into a severe depression. Over the next two years or so I attended a series of counselling sessions, moved in and out of relationships seeking relief from my seemingly hopeless state of being.

Alcohol and prescription drugs were the initial bandaids to my staying on the planet. Then I discovered meditative practices. First it was visional mindfulness Indian style practices, then I drifted to a spiritual mantra followed by focused and meditation practices, like walking barefoot on grass and feeling the earth beneath my feet, listening to the movement of the body. I did try transcendental meditation and attended counselling sessions on relaxation and loving kindness.

Finally I packed up my remaining material possessions and headed far north, living near the beach and the bush. I was void of human contact in the main, preferring to walk on the beach, do a daily ritual meditative practice then disappear in the bush and roam around all day. Bit by bit I returned to human contact. I joined a men's shed, self help group, and a walking group on a Sunday and helped out one day a week in the local aged care centre where my mother resided. I drifted into many types of other counselling sessions including sand therapy, chanting practices and joined some artists, learning to make pottery, and even drove for hours further north to attend an alternate therapy practice of placing precious stones on my body to draw out bad karma. I reckoned the practitioner just drew eighty bucks from my wallet and the session seemed a waste of time.

My evenings were alone and I wrote lots of dark poetry back then. From time to time I returned to Sydney and attended week-long live-in visual meditative practices. I had stopped drinking alcohol and went dry for a time, but when I felt better, I returned to the grog which just deepened my depression. Still depressed, I sort of worked and ultimately found a full time job and chose my own hours consulting businesses. It took a decade of rehabilitation, giving up alcohol, attending Alcoholics Anonymous and walking the Camino de Santiago and trusting in a God of my own understanding before I could let go of the negative feelings, return to health with a joyful attitude, prescription drug and alcohol free. Here are some notes to myself on the way down into the dragon's mouth which helped me with a lotus flower of creative ideas whilst recovering in rehabilitation.

Considerations for meditation:

"Acceptance of the inner core of being a loner and an outsider, as it is here (in heaven) from the inside out. Numerically I belong to the 2-3% of the population, that is three out of every hundred who fit into the cube, while others are square pegs trying to fit into the round holes. This is an enormous discovery when in the passage of time we truly accept we are born outsiders."

"Be gentle with myself, use no force, the energy will flow with me in time. Go with the grain in the wood, otherwise you will get blisters…..Go with the inner river of life."

"Go with the inner river of life, go with the flow…Put your boat of personality into the inner river of life and go with the current into open waters. Once I get the drift of this, it's just a gentle movement of the rudder to keep on course. Let it soak the marrow of your bones."

"Surrender the ego i.e. I am a little i, in name and mind."

"gradually surrender the ego- taking risks to let go and keep on letting go. I will come to a vacuum into free fall into the dragon's mouth, into the bottomless pit where the dragon lives- it will become a lotus flower of creative ideas."

"Be gentle with yourself- use no force- go with the grain of the wood- otherwise splinters."

"We may take a parachute, a crutch to lessen the fall, but be aware of the residual nervous tension remaining."

"I will know what the inner residual tensions are by the coil tensions of remaining fear, anxiety, obsessions and compulsions."

"We surrender to win, we give way to keep, we suffer to get well, we die to live-it is the opposite of what the world has to offer."

"The way is the middle road, it can't be achieved by linear, rational, sequential, logical means. Those ways are half-brained. The way of the spirit and the imagination are the third way tempered by your boat of personality floating on the river of life. Remember to adjust the rudder of existence from within my spiritual core. For we are seekers of the inner truth which becomes the universal truth."

"Surrender moment to moment to moment until I rest in thee."

"Our hearts are restless until we rest in thee."

These are just a few of the many lessons I have learnt on the way back to health and 'perceived' happiness. For I am coming to that crossroad of handing it all over to God. It is not an easy task to let go of the world in favour of God. There is still a lot of Doug at the helm of my boat of personality and not the spiritual self going with the flow. I reckon that is why I still experience sleeplessness in my will to hold on. The ultimate I know will be in the presence of God-in meditative practice, a prayer of body, feelings, awareness, loving- kindness, release, self fulfilment and non duality.

Of all the practices of meditation I have experienced, I find the most rewarding is just listening to the breath. The rhythm of breathing deep in and out in silent repetition. Right now I have ceased the practice and this is a timely reminder to return to it. For I am back to undisciplined eating habits, late nights, watching emotionally disturbing movies on Netflix, dreaming up new ideas and ultimately I have become again spiritually unsettled. It is time to stop and put back into practice the spiritual practice of meditation, attend more AA meetings for spiritual guidance and reinforce that living a sober way of life is ' a day at a time in prayerful serenity. Return again into a place of silence like a church or return to my time in the bush. It is just a matter of not thinking, just doing. And surrounding myself with like minded people.

Prayer for letting go and Acceptance.

"You are the Almighty Power to guide us on our way,
For your grace is enough,
Yes, Your grace is enough,
Your grace is enough for me. "

CHAPTER 7.

THE HEALING POWER OF A A

The unity within the fellowship of Alcoholics Anonymous is still a catalyst to enable me to recover on a daily basis from taking that next drink. I was thinking about my three Camino's in Spain, walking the pilgrimage way of St. James the Apostle of Christ who preached "Faith without works is dead" as his message to salvation whilst travelling that very same Camino Way not long after Christ's crucifixion. This has been the way of AA from its very inception. Knowing that I am a part of a miracle is a divine inspiration to me. The ability of the founders Bill Wilson and Dr. Bob Smith, working together and passing on the message to other fellowship members, tells me that to give it away is to keep it. Unity is oneness and the whole. Fellowship is for us all. Christ's message was pretty simple, "love God and thy neighbour as thyself." This is the crux of the AA fellowship-believing in a guiding light of a God of one's own understanding serving others with God's guidance .

In the 'Big Book of AA,' there is the underlying message that most alcoholics have lost their power of choice in drinking. Our so-called will power becomes practically non-existent. We are unable at certain times, to bring into our consciousness with sufficient force the memory of the suffering and humiliation of even a week or month ago. We are totally defenceless against the first drink. And once we start we can't stop by our own self will. We do not like the self searching, the levelling of our pride, the confession of our shortcomings which the process of sobriety requires for its successful consummation. But in attending AA meetings and listening to the progress of others, we come to believe in the hopelessness and futility of life as we had been living it whilst still drinking alcoholically.

So it comes to pass for all alcoholics who take on the mantle of remaining sober a day at a time, that we realise to solve our problem there is nothing left but to pick up the simple kit of spiritual tools that are laid at our feet when we join the AA fellowship. When we reach that crossroad where life is impossible, we have but two alternatives; continue to go to the bitter end, to blot out the consciousness of our intolerable situation as best we could; and the other, to accept spiritual help.

Initially what happens to most alcoholics is to accept the steps to sobriety and cling on to its message with all the desperation of a drowning man. In time it proves to be a loving power of the hand of a God of our own understanding that gives us a design for living the life of a free man or woman.

In my own case, my drinking career lasted for over four decades and whilst on the surface my success in the material world was second to none, as was my home life, I was spiritually void of love in my being. I rose to the top of my profession with proof of my value in the eyes of my peers. My marriage lasted for nearly three decades, during which time we raised and educated four children, providing the best of home life and the lavish material possessions that was in my power to provide. However, as the years went by I began to drink more and more alcoholically, getting to the point that the only way I could unwind and relax was to take another drink. It all came unstuck, the marriage broke up and the family moved on and my former pride and material possessions went out the door too. I was left to pick up the pieces. I seemed to be in a state of constant calamity that I could not find a way out of. I began to increase my intake of alcohol and ultimately collapsed in a screaming mess at a rehab for the mentally ill with addictions. It was there I realised that I was powerless over alcohol, that my life had become unmanageable and on the advice of a fellow alcoholic made my way to an AA meeting to let it wash over me. That was fifteen years ago, and I am sober a day at a time with the grace of God and the healing power of the AA programme.

So it followed that the first step of AA came crashing through to my foggy brain; that I was powerless over alcohol and my life had become unmanageable. In fact I discerned that I was not only powerless over alcohol but over people, places and things. So I began to share my story at AA meetings in a general way; what my life was like before I gave up the drink, what happened and what it is like now that I am sober. Then it came to pass that the truth dawned on me that only a power greater than self could restore me to sanity where I may serve others with unconditional love. So, like so many of my fellow AAs', I abandoned myself to the cause of the program and took the certain steps of AA as an elixir to my sobriety.

So listening to others stories and putting the steps of AA into practice we become fearless and thorough. For we realise that alcoholism is both a physical craving and a mental disease and without help we cannot stay sober. But a miracle happened to this alcoholic as it has done for millions of other alcoholics since the inception of the programme.

A God of my own understanding entered my being after six months in AA and I lost the desire for alcohol. It was then I came to embrace the healing power of AA as a guiding light to spiritual wholeness.

As it states in the AA twelve steps and traditions (pg 64) " When men and women pour so much alcohol into themselves that they destroy their lives, they commit a most unnatural act. Defying their instinctive desire for self preservation, they seem bent upon self destruction." They work against their deepest instinct. As they are progressively humbled by the terrific beating administered by alcohol, the grace of God can enter them and expel their obsession. Here their powerful instinct to live can cooperate fully with their Creator's desire to give them new life. In co-founder Bill Wilson's letters (1965) he stated: "The central characteristic of the spiritual experience is that it gives the recipient a new and better motivation out of proportion to any process of discipline, belief or faith. These spiritual experiences cannot make us whole at once; they are a rebirth to refresh a faith and certain opportunities." So it was that I began on the path of AA steps to recovery with the first step. The miracle of it all is that I let go of my ego and listened to what was on offer : "We admit we were powerless over alcohol-that our lives had become unmanageable."

My traditional belief in God did not seem to provide me with any clues to guide me in my recovery. I was off the grog, attending regular AA meetings but still in a dysfunctional state and drugged up on antidepressants. The chemical imbalance in my brain due to depression and anxiety as a result of recent tragic circumstances surrounding my life did not dissipate despite being sober. I was administered with a cocktail of drugs to level the serotonin to my brain, and despite much support from the fellowship of AA I was lost, bewildered and seemingly powerless. So at the suggestion of friends I return to rehab.

I was duty bound under the rules of the hospital to attend a 15 minute appointment per week with the resident psychiatrist. The beginnings of new found hope was presented to me by that man. I had advised him that my life was hopeless, I had no enthusiasm for living, no interest in anybody or anything and felt lost, alone and somewhat afraid. His simple response was, Congratulations Doug, you are on your spiritual path. Life will begin to change for you. You will recover in God's good time. Trust in the slow work of God." I began to attend three AA meetings a week, and after six months the desire for alcohol left me and my mood improved. In the light of a new day I found a power greater than myself to believe in. It wasn't the God of my Christian upbringing that came to my attention. It was God of my own understanding, a God of the manifest of my own creative mind. I believe now that I woke up to God in AA's Step two. "Came to believe that a Power greater than ourselves could restore us to sanity.'

It was a matter of acceptance for me that despite the unscientific nature of a mythical belief in God AA style, the miracle of it all slowly filtered into my being. Something other than the logically biblical beliefs of the God of my upbringing was filtering through; casting aside the old views and making a pathway to a new found Power greater than myself.

Those in AA who have not had a religious upbringing seemed to grasp the power of the programme more effectively in the beginning than those of us who had wandered from the faith. It seems to have come much harder for me having lost faith, rejected by God who did not answer my cries for help. Those of the roadblock of indifference, fancied self sufficiency, religious prejudice, and defiance, seem to be able to adopt and approach a logical standard to get by on. Religious people say God can be proven and happily adopt the oldest book on the subject, the Bible to endorse their philosophy of fact. The agnostic takes all the information of belief and non belief, sits on the fence with the for and against in hand sitting on the scales of justice and states God can't be proven. And the atheists simply use logical arguments claiming proof of the non-existence of God.

All the trials and tragic tribulations that overtook me had left me bewildered and diverted from the faith of my childhood. Certainly I had a good home, religious training and a code of ethics ingrained in me, and a kind of belief in God that sustained me through my former life. Besides I had alcohol to bury any unresolved issues and it seemed to be my only way through tough times. I had proof of the winning game of material success and prided myself in being hard working, honest and forthright in my day to day work ethic. The state of my soul through the majority of my life was simply a matter of confession of consciousness when I did wrong by another or became intoxicated. I just cleaned the slate, got up and moved forward again, but I never really dealt with the inner turmoil that I carried. I just buried it in the drink when I needed to and moved on. I believe that the will to win and the accolades that were bestowed upon me was proof enough that I was being of service to others and was living a good life. Of course, It was illusionary and when it all came to nothing in my great fall from grace; loss of those I perceived to love, material world of my former life and loss of faith came to pass, I discovered AA and it its healing power of God's grace.

I came to realise over time that Step two in AA is the rallying point for all of us. It matters little if one is agnostic, atheist or former believer, we can stand together on this Step. The knowledge that humility and open mindedness can lead us to faith, and every AA meeting is an assurance that God will restore us to soundness of mind if we relate ourselves to Him.

So waking up to believing in a God of greater power than yourself who could restore us to soundness of mind is one thing, but making a decision to hand our will and our lives over to the care of God as we understood him is another. To have the willingness to let God do the guiding seems foreign to us who know that we are born to free will. We decide on our own life path, our fate is in our own hands so to speak. Everything written on the subject matter seems to endorse this free will. So now that we have recognised that there is a power greater than self that runs the show, we are expected to hand over the reins to him to guide us on our way. Go into free fall and trust that he is there to catch us if we are in danger and guide us along the path he has chosen? Well, being indoctrinated into a Universal faith of belief in the birth, death and resurrection of Christ as a child and in my adult former life, the structure of that philosophy still stuck with me like scaffolding on a building. In point of fact, no matter how much I rejected the teaching of nuns and brothers in Christ, who belted the living daylight out of us in our childhood and teenage years to, indoctrinating the discipline of belief and the need to suffer like Christ did, I still carried the scars of bad karma in that regard. Besides, I had strayed so far from that part in my adult life preferring to turn to the things of the world as my method of survival to be of service to others, and live by what I had perceived as God centred.

Of course I occasionally prayed, meditated to get me through my pain and asked God for help, but it just didn't help me anymore. That is until I was confronted with step three. Then in sober mind I reasoned the logical, linear belief that the Christ of old, the crucified one, I now needed but not in the way I had been conditioned to in the past. So how was I to come to the realisation I needed an all powerful God of my own understanding to turn too? The Almighty divine to hand over to take charge of my life? How could I do that when I doubted his existence in the manner of his son Jesus Christ here on earth; his sufferings and death for the sins of man and my erroneous former life?

There and then I began to research and journal the myth and the legend of Jesus's existence as a man and as a divine son of the Father, and the grace he bestowed upon us as a gift for our salvation as an aftermath of his walk to Calvary hill and death on the cross. Through this research and journaling I came to believe in God as manifested in Jesus. I came to believe that he actually walked the earth as an Avatar- that released soul in bodily form here on earth in his time; an incarnate divine teacher, who took it upon himself to suffer and die for mankind, ascending into the heavens and siting at the right hand of his father, and belonging to the ninefold celestial hierarchy of light, adorned purity of beings. Be that myth or fact, it matters little. It is what I came to believe, take faith in and hand over to in my creative imagination. It has proved miraculous for me, for so many miracles in life have come to pass in this creative belief.

It is just as easy for me to take the stance of science and logic in an aesthetic way or indeed sit on the fence and be agnostic; but that is not what I have become. It is in the spirit of the God of the void that I exist now. I do not question, nor try to define this God-self, I simply hand over to a manifested Christ, and am guided by whatever comes up, knowing that it is in my best interest to live as the doorway of life opens or is closed for me as a consequence. Just to live it as it is, as it comes up, brings great freedom.

To put my boat of personality upon the spiritual waters of life so to speak and go with the flow is the essence of what I am about. God is the guide and I put it all out there for him, he listens and opens a door in time, and I walk through to another unknown outcome, knowing that it will all be best for me. In my journal I hold great insights as to the existence of Jesus which puts pay to any doubt I had about the reality of his being here on earth. I shall detail my journal in the next chapter but for now, a little more on the steps of AA. So it was that I began **Step 4**: " Make a searching and fearless moral inventory of ourselves." Step Four was my painstaking effort to discover what of my emotional problems I inflicted on others with misguided instinct. I wanted to find out exactly how, when and where my natural desires warped me, causing unhappiness in others, particularly as a consequence of my drinking. I learnt what my emotional deformities were and how to move forward to correct them. It had to be a searching and fearless moral inventory and without that manifested higher power in my life I doubt that I would have been as honest about it as I learnt to be.

The insight of the need for sexual gratification, material possessions to hide my insecurity and prove my worth, and the overt need for power and leadership to fill the hole of abandonment and lack of love from the heart within my life, came to the forefront. Justification of me and what I had become was hidden behind a mask of false pride, ego driven behaviour, and the drowning of my spiritual essence in alcoholic behaviour. For in taking an inventory of my defects of character, I knowingly was gaining a gift of humility. At least to some degree, for I was of the depressive and power driven personality of extremes, of which the world abounds. The fourth step had me find the shoes that best b fitted my personality; defined what my defects of character are and learn to walk with confidence to at last be on the right track. I had a moral inventory to ponder and then it was time to take the next step.

Step Five: "Admit to God, to ourselves, and to another human being the exact nature of our wrongs." I had found a simple way of writing the wrongdoings to share with an older sober member in the fellowship. I simply wrote down in no particular order the names only of people I had wronged in my former alcoholic lifetime. Once I had my list, I went back over the list, quantified the nature of my defect that I sort to 'confess' and how I was willing to let go, defuse myself of the karma of it all and moved forward freely with the grace of God. I then chose an older sober member whom I had come to know over the years of my sobriety and asked him if I could share my step five with him. He has since died after suffering from cancer. He died gracefully and I realised at his funeral how he had kept his ego in check. It was related in the epilogue of his life; he lived a successful life in the eyes of the world that he never spoke of. For he had something very special and rewarding that I now try to emulate taking a leaf out of his book. He never boasted of his achievements, he was humble to the core and very giving of himself to others.

I sat with him (my guiding light of the moment) to share my fifth step. He placed an empty chair opposite me and stated: "Doug, you are not sharing these incidents of your life with me only, you are sharing them with God. Imagine he is in that empty chair and direct all you have to share with him, for I am just here to listen and observe." Once I had detailed all the errors of my ways, mostly relating to my lack of a moral compass whilst under the influence of alcohol and mean spiritedness to my family, and let them go in my head, my friend of the moment gave me one other piece of advice that I did as soon as I had finished my sharing of admission of the exact nature of my wrongs. I made my way into the bush with the paper I had written my character defects upon, dug a hole, lit a match and burned it all to cinders. Then I buried it and left it all behind me.

I was moved to let the God of my own understanding, remove all my defects of character as in **Step 6**. I was now at the beginning of the best possible attitude to life that I could muster. It would be a long journey but I was 'entirely ready' to have God progressively remove my shortcomings. Sure it would not happen overnight, but with a persistent habit to improve, I would (will) learn to let go and change for the purpose in life God intends for me from now on. I needed to ask him humbly to remove my shortcomings (**Step 7**) and continue to make a list of persons in my life I had harmed, and become willing to make amends to them all, be they living or dead. (**Step 8**).

The fact that followed was the decision to make direct amends wherever possible, except when to do so would injure them or others. This is the essence of **Step 9** and it requires good judgement, a careful sense of timing, and a mustering of courage, the wisdom of caution and common sense before taking the decision to make amends. For many of those to whom I needed to make amends have long ago moved on, have 'gone to God' or would not relish any contact with me after such a long time. It might prove more troubling to them if I made contact and apologised for my past behaviour. I had to evaluate if I would do a face to face contact wherever I could, or write a letter and post it, or perhaps write a letter of apology, and burn it like I had done in my fifth step.

Most Saturday mornings you will find me at the same AA meeting. It is run on the theme of what happened in your life in the past week centred around **Step10** ``Continued to take personal inventory and when we were wrong promptly admitted it." **Step 11**; "Sought through prayer and meditation to improve our conscious contact with God as we understood Him, praying only for knowledge of His will for us and the power to carry that out." And **Step 12:** "Having had a spiritual awakening as a result of these steps, we tried to carry this message to alcoholics, and to practise these principles in all our affairs."

When it comes to Step 10 it is fair to say that we all fall down due to our defects of character on a daily basis. When it comes to those within and outside the program, we more often than not are possessed by pride, anger, envy, laziness or some other defect in our day to day dealings with others. The Step 10 continuing to take personal inventory helps us to become spiritually aware when we are wrong and we can simply forgive ourselves and as quickly as is practical confront those we have offended and promptly admit our offence and apologise. If we are not taking an inventory in writing then a daily examination of consciousness as it relates to offending others can be done in the evening. It's best if we don't let the sun go down on any matter where we are wrong. At least a phone call before going to bed to make the apology or sending a text saying you're sorry for your wrongdoing will turn the bad karmic effect on oneself into good karma and grace from God in the form of love for others and especially for one's own peace of mind.

 I am not saying I do this every day but at least once a week at that AA meeting recalling my past week centred on Steps 10, 11 and 12 brings everything back into focus. Step 11 is self fulfilling if we put it into practice too. When I was going through the worst of my depression and anxiety, having given up the drink as band aid to my suffering heart, I meditated regularly. As mentioned in a previous chapter I tried every type of meditation known to man. Ultimately though deep breathing and just listening to my breath is the best sound to quieten my chattering mind. When all seems right sized in my life I fall back into old habits, cease meditation and prayer and find myself back at square one. The warning signs are sleepless nights, going to bed too late, watching late night violent movies, using food to substitute for spiritual wholeness, 'care-less-ness' for others when giving my ego a boost and lack of prayer and meditation. This is why the Saturday meeting is good for me, it brings me back in line to a routine of a few quiet prayers, meditation, listening to my body in early morning yoga practice and getting to meetings more regularly. And spending quiet time seated in an empty church being in the present, or dare I say the presence of God, be that in the symbols of what the Church is adorned with or what is in my imagination.

Some Protestants believe that catholics pray to Mary, the Mother of Jesus and consider this not to be in keeping with Christian belief of going direct to jesu fro guidance in prayer and meditation. Well, I never found it to be so. In fact to the best of my recollection growing up in a Catholic faith, we were taught to pray not 'to' mary but 'through' mary to intercede to her son on our behalf. Much like he parade of Jesus changing water into wine at the marriage feast of Cana. His first miracle that has been recorded in the New testament. Mary simply said something like " Son they have not wine " So Jesus as dutiful son y turned water into wine to appease his mother's wishes. In much the same way catholics approach mary, the mother of Jesus in prayer for their own special intention.

The prayer that follows s a traditional prayer of request to Mary to ask Jesus for an answer via His Mother for a special intention. It can easily be misconstrued by those not conditioned to the Catholic faith to misunderstand this prayer. Suffice to say that it is a personal choice who a believer prays to or through to maintain a healthy loving heart and peace of mind.

The Memorare.

Remember O most gracious Virgin Mary,

that never was it known that anyone who fled

to thy protection, implored they help, or

sought thine intercession was left unaided.

Inspired with confidence, I fly to thee,

O Virgin of virgins, my mother, to thee do I

come, before thee I stand, sinful and

sorrowful. O Mother of the Word Incarnate,

despise not my petition, but in thy mercy

hear and answer me.

                                        Amen

CHAPTER 8.

A GOD OF LOGIC AND THE MANIFEST

It is both the Church symbolism and the Risen Christ, the God of the Manifest, that keeps me of sober mind and of spiritual duties in logical acceptance and imaginary observance of faith in a power greater than self. A Tabernacle on the altar from my Christian upbringing is a representation of the Jewish Temple and the slaughter of the lamb performed by a layman, followed by the rituals dealing with the blood and fat which had to be carried out by a priest in the Jewish historical tradition. The priest in turn cooked the flesh of the lamb on the altar and the smoke essence that rose from the cooking to the heavens above was an observance of the assembly in worship. They were given the flesh of the lamb to eat as a symbol of their faith. In much the same way Christ reportedly offered himself as a living sacrifice for the sin of man, and the body and blood of Christ is kept in the form of a bread and wine and eaten by the faithful in commemoration of Christ's living sacrifice. The Tabernacle of the Catholic faith, if you will, symbolises the Jewish temple altar of the old testament and Christianity is the new Judaism.

So too, the Stations of the Cross around the walls of the church tell the story of Christ's ordeal for mankind, as do the statues of the Virgin Mary and the saints. Even the church and its architecture has that symbolism. As I was educated to this, or rather indoctrinated to it in my youth, it is natural for me to gain some peace in such a place without necessarily following the religion of my youth. It is as if the logic of the symbols and signs of my former faith have a head justification of a belief in the Higher Power, but my creative brain sees the God particle as a manifested Christ who is risen, and in whom I can hand over to. But how did I arrive at this having turned agnostic for many years in my adult life, and for a little while reached a scientific come atheistic cynical view of non belief. Well, it was when I could no longer take the itch that I could not scratch to align me with the Third Step of AA that I knew I needed a Higher Power to embrace.

So it was that I began to research the reality of the actual existence of Christ on earth some two thousand years ago. I wanted to believe again without reservation. I needed to prove some semblance of truth to embrace to live the Steps of AA, to hang my hat on so to speak, to live in my own acceptance of a Power greater than self. A guiding light to help me remain sober, to meditate with and pray to in my recovery, to help other still suffering alcoholics remain sober a day at a time. Then it was that I turned to historic records, biblical reference, the gospels of Mathew, Mark, Luke and John in the way of other faiths as they related to Jesus and the in depth written references of great scholars and philosophers throughout history.

The belief and non belief in the birth, death and Resurrection and Ascension of Christ has comparative myth and fact. As far back as the ancient Mayan recording and interpretations of the sky, was the belief that the will and actions of the Gods could be read in the Stars, Moon and Planets. The Maya believed that the Earth was the centre of all things, fixed and immovable. The stars, the Moon, Sun, and the planets were Gods. These planetary 'Gods' and their movements were seen as going between earth, the underworld, and other celestial destinations. These Gods were greatly involved in human affairs and their movement was watched closely. Certain traceless moments like a war or a mighty ruler's ascent to the throne would be delayed or advanced only when a certain planet was visible in the sky. In much the same way, the ancient Aboriginal culture told stories from ancient Gods, animals and plant growth patterns. With perhaps one exception, the Aborigine retold these stories through to the 20th century, of the birth of a certain God, who had a son from a black star in the skies, the son star died and left a spirit star for the tribes to follow. That star being the 'Evening Star' which is the brightest star forever more in the eastern skies of Australia.

Ultimately, the Maya ascertained that the Sun was the most powerful of all the planet Gods, and would shine in the sky all day before transforming into a Jaguar at night and passing through the Mayan underworld. It was the Maya who recorded the Sun dying (eclipse) in the sky to remain then in the underworld for three days before rising again in a new spiritual realism. Like man before and after the Mayan dynasties, who often claimed they descended from the Moon but worshipped the Sun, their most important planet was Venus, which was associated with battles and wars. Captured warriors and leaders would be sacrificed according to the position of Venus in the night sky. The Maya painstakingly recorded the movements of Venus and determined the year, relative to the Earth and not the Sun, was 584 days long, amazingly close to the 583.92 days that modern science has determined, when using a similar trajectory.

Moving from the misunderstandings of the 'Gods' of the ancients, and their myths of belief in a Sun God, the questions of copy-cat biblical stories of the Christ is nothing more than a plagiarist repeat of the stories of Horus, Krishna, Mithras, Dionysus and other pagan Gods, retold up to the time of the Roman 'God' Octavian. Octavian, later called Caesar Augustus, perpetrated a myth to keep a rabble distracted, alluding to the belief that he, 'Augustus' was the real Christ, the 'Sacrifice lamb' of the peoples of the Roman Empire and the Jewish 'heathen.' He, who would be adored as the one true God and everlasting in their lives and the hereafter.

It has been considered by modern day writings, possibly totally mythical, that Augustus, the then Roman leader Caesar Augustus, after the murder of his foster father Julius Caesar, had scribes record the myth of himself being 'Messiah.' He manufactured the story, having Saul, a Roman soldier, go forth and recruit followers after his so-called 'conversion' on the road to Damascus. If one was to believe such a 'story'- this may have occurred before Christ's ascension into heaven. However, the Bible in Acts, clearly indicates Saul (St.Paul's) conversion occurred well after the Ascension. It is a moot point and really is essentially trivia: a case of the story of Christ on earth can not be proven or disproven, much less the case for Caesar Augustus being the true Messiah! There is more documented evidence, in the Bible and other credible recorded literature that confirms the reality of the Christ on earth story. Myth or reality, modern day man is either a believer or a disbeliever. I have my doubts about a living Christ on earth but stand to be corrected. A living Christ is an inward thing, I have come to accept this as a belief. Be it Christ in the manifest of Roman times, Christ in the biblical account that pacifies the brain of traditional believers or a Christ of one's own imagination is not the concern. The dead Christ can only, to my mind, be a Christ of the imagination, of an inner consciousness- a manifestation, whatever realm of belief one chooses to follow.

It is not my task here to throw out the baby with the bathwater, but merely do my best to grow an embryonic manifestation of the Christ spirit for myself and give you, dear reader, words to consider on this subject. My writings here occurred well after my return to Australia from my third Camino. As I had previously stated, my mind of The Way was a healing mind, an enquiring mind and a mind of a sceptic wanting to believe in something other than what the world I grew up in and indeed the current material world, other than what a "'Santiago Travelling wanderer" has to offer. So the text surrounding the signs of the zodiacs, the parallels relating to past spiritual leaders, doctrinaires of faith and morals, the signs in the planets, in the end count for little more than a puff of smoke in the reality of the now. I guess I begin to see what Christ reportedly said "The kingdom of heaven is within." When one deconstructs the Christ of miracle, mystery and authority, it is a short step to wondering if the whole story of Christ is a myth. Thinking on that premise, and the deepest construct of a creative human spirituality, the historical Jesus, as such never existed.

However, very few of history and biblical studies draw the conclusion that a Jesus of the old story never existed. The main division in scholastic concerns is how to appropriate Jesus. Was he an apocalyptic or a wisdom-centred teacher? Few researchers question if he ever lived. Still, on a popular level, Jesus, understood as a myth, and strictly a myth, seems to be gaining ground. So, was he or wasn't he? Did he ever live or is it all just a good story? Critical examination of Christian gospels, especially with the rise of formal criticism, does recommend the conclusion that Jesus as the centre of Christian dogma emerged in the itinerant preaching of the earliest Jesus movement.

Basically, people spoke in the manner of the 'living' Jesus who had died. Preachers spoke 'in the spirit of Jesus,' thus making him alive in their witness. The Gospel of John is historical in the sense that it records the 'speaking in the spirit of Jesus.' This was the charisma of the early Church which, of course, eventually needed to be regulated in some form. The earliest social movements related to Jesus preserved his memory in this way. The parables and aphorisms of Jesus are a case in point. The forms of speech of this 'historic' Jesus, a base mode of teaching, was preserved, if re-interpreted, in the teaching and preaching of the next generation. Formal criticism was all about finding the voiceprint of the teacher that carried forward in new shapes, by students of this form. Now comes the myth. It all starts by asking how much of the Jesus material is fictional, arising from later generations who spoke 'In the name of Jesus' without actually saying anything the historical Jesus said. Also, how much of the Jesus material can be identified with confidence as an originating voice point, something close to historical? The line between these two questions is often blurry, and it is exactly this blurriness that inspires the possibility that all the material is mythical, that is, all the material is made up 'in the name of Jesus.' Once that step is taken, the natural conclusion is that there is no historical Jesus. It is actually hard to prove there was a historical Jesus using conventional forms of history. Jesus was unknown. We have to remember that the big name of his lifetime was Socrates. Everybody, including Jesus, had heard of Socrates. He was famous. Jesus, as a Galilean of his time was not famous and had no chance as his birth right of ever being famous. In the light of the rise of Christianity it is hard to imagine that Jesus was an unknown. He may have been illiterate and poor as was his community. No one was able to hire scribes to read great works to them, to record great thoughts or send letters home. Still he was a carpenter's son so he would have perhaps understood mathematics and his reported knowledge of preaching to the scribes in the temple proves he was not ignorant. The Christian gospels record that the popularity of Jesus and his large following is almost certainly imaginary. His crucifixion by the Roman authorities was done without blinking-another nobody in a long line of nobody rabble rousers. We look at Jesus from the perspective of 2000 years of history and he seems to us to be among the greats. Indeed, he is amongst the greats, but in the immediate experience of his life he belongs to a minor school or movement that was largely ignored and mostly unknown. Accordingly, it is not possible to expect a great recovery of contemporary witness to his life and times.

What we can expect is second-and third-generation historians mentioning him in light of a new and rising movement that claims him as the true Caesar (the Lord, Saviour, and the Son of God). Ancient historians and those not so ancient questioned: who was this Jesus and who were his people? Later historians know about the rising movement and relay whatever information they can gather regarding its founder. The information is humble. It concerns the followers who called him 'The Christ.' his relationship to another teacher named John the Baptist, that he was crucified, that his followers are poor and ignorant. That there were lies and rumours spread about him. This is what we can read in Josephus, Tacitus, Suetonius, the letter of Pliny the Younger and others Mar-ben Saparion, Lucian and Samosata to name but a few of the many. So why then does the idea that Jesus never was persist and gain in popular assent? The answer is plain fact that despite the aforementioned, there is no contemporary witness to the Jesus of history. The earliest we can get is Paul, an educated Roman soldier, who said that Jesus was once historical (2 Cor 5:16) who met and knew 'the brother of the Lord.' (Gal 1:19). Still, it remains simply true that there has never been an eyewitness report about any incident in the life of Christ. This simple fact is often the foundation for believing Jesus was only purely a myth.The second element that supports the belief Jesus was a myth emerges because this belief is partially correct. Much about Jesus is indeed a myth.

Really, much about anybody, including our own self is mythical. With Jesus, like with Confucius or other ancient teachers about whom nothing really exists, myth comes with the package. The earliest Christian movement did interpret Jesus in the light of Jewish scripture; especially the prophets. The dying and rising of Jesus is consistent with the notion of divine intervention in pagan Gods, biblical reference-where the notion of regeneration is prevalent. Jesus, his death and resurrection, fits right in with these common, and universal, mythical patterns.

Early educated Christians could draw upon both Jewish, Greek and later Roman sources in this regard. Thirdly, it is a plain fact that many early Christian preachers spoke in the name of Jesus, saying things that Jesus never said. Christianity created a cache of Jesus sayings that contained both historical and non-historical inspired sayings about the nature of Jesus, his divinity and the realm of the Kingdom of God. Whilst the commentary on the parables is made up, the use of parables is not. Jesus never said 'I and the Father are one.' (John 10:30) but rather he used parables like 'a sower went out to sow his seed.' (Mark 4:3). and Mark did interpret the sower parable as an allegory about the quality of Christian believers.

So, even within the Christian sources that witness Jesus, much of the witness is myth. There is not much any historian can do about this situation except to understand it. Still, it does not prove the case that Jesus never existed. We all want something to believe, and sometimes when we used to feel certain about becoming questionable, the reaction is to throw the whole thing out. I guess I felt this way in the year my whole world seemed to come unhinged. I believed many things about my life from childhood to adulthood that turned out to be a myth. It all seemed to unravel in one year, some 20 years ago. In that year there was a complete breakdown of my family tree. A long standing marriage was desecrated to the dust, as was tragedy to befall me and mine. A wedge between young and old took an evil hold and I stood by and watched the fruits of my labour, my then perceived reason for living, wither on the vine. When I recovered from my sadness and madness, I discovered in my new adulthood things about myself and my family, my then value system that was all myth. I discovered that the mantra I lived by, the code of ethics I subscribed to, the 'story' I had told myself since childhood to get by and survive to a great degree were not true. In fact I had been, to a large degree living a myth without recognising it as such. The human truth of the Jesus I was taught to believe as a child varied greatly to the Jesus that now evolves within.

When does the historical Jesus become someone who can inspire us and teach us about life outside Christian myth? This involves, and perhaps is the consequence of the act of forgiving Jesus for being human. It is part of his fate, to be one of the greatest myths of human history. But this does not erase the voiceprint of a historical figure.

True, it makes Jesus an enigma, but it does not eliminate the basic fact of his humanity. So on the scales of belief, my own and by further investigation, like an anthropologist digging up some unidentified bones and trying to make some sense of the find, I endorse it. Not so much from a historical aspect but from agreement of factual verification of believers.

I began to journal down some beliefs that have evolved over the centuries in support of what Winston Churchill stated about Russia at the end of WWII- 'It is a riddle, wrapped in a mystery, inside an enigma.' Mine being more an endorsement to the existence of Christ breaking the riddle, unwrapping the mystery, which leans to fact more than fiction or enigma. God throughout the Bible spoke through the prophets to prove he was God. He foretold the future through them to verify who he was, to prove to people that those who spoke were true prophets, and to draw mankind to worship him only. The 100% accuracy of the prophecies that can be uncovered in the Bible that came true are proof of the existence of God and of Jesus if one opens the mind to these documented proofs.

'I am God, and there is none like me. Declaring the end from the beginning, and from ancient times the things that are not yet done saying, 'My counsel shall stand, and I will do all my pleasure:' (Isaiah 46: 10-11). There are many hundreds of predictions that have come true from the time of Christ, 30 AD until today. Perhaps the most pertinent right now are those that relate to Russia and the nations of Islam. Predicted ca. 10th Century BC: psalm 120:5-7 predicted that Russia and Arabia would be a people that hate peace and embrace War. Fulfilled in 600 AD to the present for Arabia: when the Arabian prophet Muhammad spread his new religion of Islam, he used wars to do it and his followers have been warring ever since. Russia is still warring today but the ultimate war will come in the future as prophesied in Ezekiel 38-39, when they will lead a group of nations to fight Israel. It is to be hoped that the request of Our Lady of Fatima to pray for the conversation of Russia in this 21st century will stave off this biblical prophecy. It is to be hoped that Vladimir Putin, if he retains power in Russia, will be a prayerful catalyst to help save the planet from a pending Nuclear War and not continue on his present course towards Armageddon.

One must hope as a non believer that this comes to pass and as a believer, that Putin is not living a KGB deception using the old Russian Orthodox Church as a cover for an even bigger future plot. Let us trust that he returns to being a man of prayer that he seems to adjudicate by his actions within the

Orthodox Church. The past biblical predictions do not leave one with much comfort for the future. Perhaps the predictions of Christ that have come to pass will give some reassurance to this doubting Thomas and to other pilgrims of the road of life towards eternity. Jesus reportedly, did not only fulfil prophecy in his own lifetime, he predicted coming events that were to come to pass in the future. One of the ministries of Jesus was that of the prophet. As has been true with prophecies fulfilled in his lifetime, his prophetic words have been literally and marvellously fulfilled!

Here I was back on the road again on another Camino. Trudging once more the well worn pathway to Santiago de Compostela. I was somewhere north west of the City of Leon, and stopped at Villar de Mazarife, at a small cafe on the side of the Way; some 21 km journey was more than enough for me for that day. It was mid afternoon and still quite hot. Finishing my cup of coffee I made my way to a nearby church to meditate. In the cool of a chapel of God, I reached into my backpack, consulting my journal of notes I had taken that day for a quick review. Certainly I had written copious jottings on the historic Christ on earth and fulfilled predictions of the existence of God the Father, but had I justified the spiritual Christ reality?

I knew I would review and expand on my writings with further research on my return to Australia from this Camino journey. But, on a scale of judgement of myself, had I reviewed enough of the Christ reality to balance the scales between belief and non belief; sitting in my lofty heights of self-righteousness reading between the lines. Indeed, what of the proof of Christ's existence, his predictions and his miracles? For that matter, what of the life and times of his disciple James the Stronger, who reportedly walked The Way I now trod? A story I didn't really believe but had made a note to further investigate, like I now planned to do on Jesus on my return home. I figured I still had a long way to go to rest my case, as I needed to rest my weary head, on my way to Santiago. Once more to journey to the end of the Way, out of darkness into light? To visit the Cathedral where I had first had my doubts about St. James ever visiting Spain let alone preach of his leader Jesus the Nazarene. At the Cathedral, despite my doubts, I had confessed my wrong doings, received absolution from a priest and had eaten the Communion host. Yet, I had returned to that Cathedral on my second Camino in a worse spiritual state than my first, with no thought of forgiveness in my heart, no participation in the midday Mass ceremony. Just the thought of returning to a wayward woman of the Camino for a final fling.

The closest I got to a spiritual experience in that Cathedral and on the Way was to once more to visit the crypt of St. James under the altar of the Santiago Cathedral, put my arms around a statue of his image above the altar and spend my time in Santiago investigating the purpose of the Mass, the Ark of the Covenant, and the host of Christ in communion. Investigating the 'smoke- belcher ' ceremony and the reverence that one might hold for the reenactment of Christ's last supper in the Mass and the golden Tabernacle on the Altar.

A typical investigation of one with no belief let alone a doubting Thomas, who once had been educated Catholic, once wore the arm of the courage of my convictions and the shield of Christ protection from sin. My current state was perhaps worse than my first and my second visit to the Cathedral, for I was lost in a time and a space warp, somehow in a void between the fantasy and the reality of a Christ-like existence. I resolved to do more research on this Christ figure, on St. James reported life and purpose on the Camino, to see if I could swing the scales of Judgement more to a justice of belief than unbelief, to perhaps renew the courage of my former faithful convictions or to drop the whole bundle as a useless exercise. Did Christ really exist? Where is the proof from non-Bible sources that he is real? These questions and others like it are often asked by Bible sceptics and atheists alike.

Could I uncover historical facts from secular sources as well as Christian, that Jesus was real and existed? Also that he is the most documented and historically verifiable figure in antiquity? I had done a fair job in my journal on God the Father, I thought, now how about his son? To get real verification, I turned once more to the library of words in sacred manuscripts and books I had purchased in bookshops and carried with me on this now more realistic inward journey of the Way. I first turned to Josephus, who did not believe Jesus was the son of God, but who wrote about him. I decided to work my way through the many secular historians who lived in the century after the death of Jesus who confirmed his existence, Flavius Josephus being the first.

Titus Flavius Josephus (37-c.100), a first Century Roman-Jewish historian and hagiography of priestly ancestry recorded Jewish history, with special emphasis on the 1st Century AD and the First Jewish-Roman War, which resulted in the Destruction of Jerusalem and its temple in 70 AD. His most important works recount the history of the world from a Jewish perspective for an ostensibly Roman audience. These works provide valuable insight into 1st Century Judaism and the background of Early Christianity. Josephus was a

Jew who did not believe in Jesus Christ as the Son of God or Christianity. In 'The Antiquities of the Jews', book 18, chapter 3, paragraph 3 this famous historian writes: "Now there was about this time Jesus, a wise man, if it is lawful to call him a man, for he was a doer of wonderful works- a teacher of such men as receive the truth with pleasure. He drew over to him both many of the Jews, and many of the Gentiles. He was (the) Christ; and when Pilate, at the suggestion of the principal men amongst us, had condemned him to a cross......" Josephus goes on with further proof as to the condemnation of Christ. Josephus, considered one of the greatest historians of antiquity, independently provided proof and evidence of Christ's reality confirming the biblical account as well.

Cornelius Tactus was a Roman Historian who lived from 55-120 AD and wrote the following passage that refers to Jesus, called 'Christ', which means 'The Messiah', in book 15, chapter 44 of The Annals. After a six day fire burned much of Rome: "Consequently, to get rid of the report, Nero fastened the guilt and inflicted the most exquisite tortures on a class hated as an abomination, called Christians by the populace. Christ from whom the name had its origin, suffered the most extreme of penalties during the reign of Tiberius at the hands of procurator, Pontius Pilatus." Titus goes on to describe how the followers of Christ like him perished. Despite the fact that clearly despised Christianity as a 'mischievous superstition', Tacitus no less confirms once again the existence of Jesus and his crucifixion on the cross, it also states Pontius Pilate as the procurator who oversaw the crucifixion again giving non- Biblical proof of Jesus' existence as it is recorded in the Bible.

Plinius the Younger wrote of the Persecution of Christians. Gaius Plinius Cascilius Secundus, (61AD –112 AD) better known as 'Pliny, The Younger' was a lawyer, author and magistrate of Ancient Rome. He wrote numerous letters to such notables as Tacitus and the Emperor Trajan. He was considered an honest and moderate man, consistent in pursuit of suspected Christian members according to Roman law, and rose through a series of Imperial civil and military offices, the cursus honorum- imperial sequential order of office. In correspondence with the Emperor Trajan he reported on his actions against the followers of Christ. He asks the Emperor for instructions dealing with Christians and explained he forced Christians to curse Christ under painful torture. So not only was Pliny aware of Jesus Christ, he also provided a description of the activities of the early Church. In later writings he details persecution against Christians.

Sextus Julius Africanus (c.160-c. 240) was a Christian traveller and historian of the late 2rd and early 3rd century AD. He is important chiefly because of his influence on Eusebius, on all the late writers of Church history among the Fathers, and on the Greek school of chroniclers. Julius Africanus quotes about writings of Thallus, who was the first non– Christian historian. In his Chronicles, Africanus quoting the historian Thallus, explains the reason for it being so dark during the time of the day of the crucifixion of Jesus Christ: 'an eclipse of the sun.' Non- Christian proof of Jesus' existence and another confirmation of the Bible's account of Jesus crucifixion.``

The Bible states a reference to the time Jesus was put on the cross which is confirmed here: 'now from the sixth hour there was darkness over all the land until the ninth hour.' The sixth hour is noon and the ninth hour 3 P.M. Thus we see that the historian Thallus was trying to explain the odd occurrence of the sky being dark at noon at the time of the crucifixion of Jesus as an eclipse. Africanus also quoted Phlegon, a Greek historian who lived in 2nd century AD and also wrote of the eclipse occurring on the day Jesus was crucified. This again confirms non Christian sources that confirm the account of Jesus being a real person who lived as well as confirming the account of his crucifixion straight from the bible. And another bible quote: 'At the death of Christ, the sun darkened , the earth trembled and the dead arose and appeared to many.'

Lucian (Born 115 AD) was a well known Greek satirist and a travelling lecturer. More than eighty works bear his name. He mocked Christians in his writing, but at the same time provided evidence that Jesus was real. 'He was second only to that one whom they worship today, the man in Palestine who was crucified because he brought this new form of initiation into the world.' He goes on to describe the belief of Christians, the personal sacrifices they make, their transgression from denying Greek Gods to worship this Christian God. And being all on one level with this God in their belief for eternity. Lucian does not mention Christ by name but he confirms his existence that he was crucified in 'Palestine', had followers who believed in eternal life and that they were equal in Jesus Christ. Lucian even mentions that Christians deny all other gods and believe in 'faith alone.' This again is in accordance with the Bible's clear statements about the Christian faith and provides more evidence of the existence of Christ, that 'the man in Palestine, did really exist.'

Gaius Suetonius Tranquillus, known as Suetonius (ca.69-75)-was a Roman historian belonging to the equestrian order era in the early Imperial era. His most important surviving work is a set of biographies of twelve successive Roman rulers from Julius Caesar to Domitian, entitled 'De Vita Caesarum'. In the apparent description of his writing he states- 'The Emperor Claudius reigned 41AD to 54 AD.' Suetonius reports his dealings with the Eastern Roman Empire, that is, with Greece and Macedonia, and with Lycian, Rhodesians, and Trojans. He then reports that the Emperor expelled Jews from Rome, since they 'constantly made disturbances at the instigation of Christ.' Sceptics will point to the different spelling to say that's not the Jesus he's talking about. But again, with the totality of evidence, it's obvious that followers of Jesus in the Roman Empire were persecuted by Roman authorities. It certainly falls in line with other chronicles and biblical historical parchments that the Romans who followed Jesus were being punished for it.

There is a great logical fallacy among Bible sceptics, atheists and those who challenge Christianity that says, when discussing historical aspects of the Bible 'you can't use the Bible as proof that Jesus existed. You use non-Bible sources!' To which this author says 'Well, why not?' The four Gospels of the Bible are bibliographical accounts of the life of Jesus. The normal objective measure of the reliability of historical documents is..1) The number of available copies of ancient manuscript. 2.) The time span between original versions and the date of those copies are still in existence today. When examined under this standard, the Bible proves to provide a treasure trove of proof and evidence that Jesus really existed. All other non-biblical historical evidence supports and reinforces this. Manuscript fragments of the New Testament documents, written between 50-100 AD, support all the biblical and non-biblical evidence of the existence of Jesus Christ. The record of life, ministry, death and resurrection of Jesus Christ has more evidence and proof than any other person from antiquity. Jesus believed that he was just a regular man but he was reportedly the Son of God, who gave his life on the cross that so many historians knew about, to take the punishment for the wrongdoings of humanity. It takes faith and trust in that sacrifice to receive him. Jesus said: "Behold, I stand at the door, and knock: if any man hears my voice, and opens the door, I will come in to him, and will sup with him, and he with me. To him that over-cometh will I grant to sit with me in my throne, even as I also overcame and I sit down with my Father in his throne."- 11 Revelation 3: 20-21.

Jesus obviously wants us to believe in him based on volumes of documented evidence of his birth, death, resurrection, ascension into heaven. If we are to be free from our defects of character, we have to be committed in our lives here and now to have eternal life in the hereafter and reign with him. So now that it is established that He existed, what is it that he is really asking of us? I began to ponder this thought. Still determined to further delve into the matter of faith now and not the evidence of his existence. Did I really need to do that though? What is it that this God of my inner spirit is asking of me? I was thinking. Jesus in the scriptures particularly the Sermon on the Mount, in Matthew's gospel points out the essence of his teaching: Jesus is consistently seen to be merciful, gracious, faithful, forgiving, and steadfast in love. Of course, it is not always easy on a daily basis to live by this Credo.

But if Jesus is the image of his Father i.e. the Universal God figure that is nonetheless hard to believe in his existence in the void, and we are called to imitate him then it stands to reason that the way to live by these principles is to bring those five adjectives into play. So practising mindfulness as Christ dictated in his Sermon on the Mount is to appreciate the need for his grace- that gift that can only be absorbed by doing unto others as they would have us do unto you. Those five adjectives of mercy, grace, faith, forgiveness and steadfastness seem to be the catalyst of human action for the betterment of oneself and our fellow man. If that's all there is to it, then it's worth a shot to try this Christ credo for a better life- being a believer or a non believer. Jesus was only on earth as a man for a short time. He was visited by shepherds as a witness to his coming for they had been told already by an angel of his birth. Likewise Magi Kings had followed a star from the east to the place of his birth:, offering gifts of gold, frankincense and myrrh.

So what have we got from history and the Bible as a template 'proof' to follow the way of this man called Jesus? Apart from his preaching to the priests of the temple at age 12, he goes missing for 18 years and next appears when he returns from 40 day fasting in the desert and is baptised by John the Baptist in the river Jordan. He preaches for the next three years to his followers performs many miracles, predicted future events, and ultimately sacrificed himself on the cross for the wrongdoings of mankind, died and was buried at age 33, rose again from the dead three days later, visited his followers and ascended into the heavens. Jesus not only fulfilled his own spoken prophecy in his lifetime, he predicted events that were to come to pass some time in the future. One of the ministries was that of a prophet. Jesus had predicted that 'heaven and earth will pass away, but my words will not pass away' (Mathew 24:35)-to date his words still echo throughout Christendom, read and be lieved by untold millions. Mary of Bethany poured oil on the body of Jesus in her anticipation of his death. She was rebuked by the disciples for wasting the oil. Jesus chastised them saying that her story would be retold wherever the gospel was preached.This has always come to pass.

Jesus also predicted that one of his own would betray him. This was literally fulfilled by Judas. Jesus predicted that Peter would deny him three times before the cock crowed. This too came to pass. He predicted that he would suffer at the hands of religious rulers. On the night he was arrested the religious rulers allowed him to be beaten. Jesus predicted he would die in Jerusalem and upon a cross. Both predictions took place. He predicted that he would die during the Passover and would rise again in three days. This is well documented as having occurred as he predicted.

Many other events such as the destruction of the City of Jerusalem within one generation, the destruction of the Temple, the scattering of the Jewish people from their land, their captivity and the ruling of the Holy land by the Gentiles, the persecution of the Jewish people and though persecuted, the nation of Jews would survive-all of these predictions have been literally fulfilled. These facts demonstrate beyond any doubt that Jesus was indeed a genuine prophet. During his earthly ministry Jesus touched and transformed countless lives. Like other events in the life of Jesus, all his miracles were documented by eyewitnesses. The Gospels record 37 of these and are mentioned in various texts by the four writers Mathew, Mark, Luke and John. The ability at age 12 to interpret holy scriptures and teach wise scribes and priests in the Temple of Jerusalem would seem like a miracle to them at the time.

He went on to perform many miracles over the remaining 3 years of his remaining time on earth before he was crucified. This was followed by healing the sick, casting out evil spirits from the possessed, cleansing those diseased; restoring the use of limbs, restoring the sight of the blind and hearing of the deaf; calming the sea, ensuring a major fish catch, feeding the multitude, walking on water, bringing people back to life and many more.

So it was that I came to believe and relive the logic of the symbolism of the Church teachings of my youth without actually embracing the Church, and to learn to hand over and trust in a manifested Christ of my own understanding in the creative imagination. To this day, this trust has worked as an untold miracle for me in the handing over to that power. "I" off me so to speak, and the healing power of AA has helped me stay sober a day at a time to the present day. Others may have a Buddhist view as their Higher Power, some may have the Almighty God of Mohammad's message to cling too, still others may have view of the reality of nature as their guiding power, whilst some may simply depend on the healing Power of AA in any meeting or some may well struggle sitting on the fence so to speak and are as yet to embrace a Higher power. It is not for me to judge, but it is my job to trust in what I embrace as a Higher Power, within the Steps of AA and in particular Steps 3: letting go and handing over to the God of my understanding and Step 11; Meditation and prayer in my conscious contact with God, and Step 12 having had a spiritual awakening, try to carry the AA message to other still suffering alcoholics .

'If there's a secret I could whisper and you could keep. It's that it's all inside you already, every single thing you need.'

-The afterlife of Billy Fingers.

CHAPTER 9.

PERSONAL STORIES

The Big Book, The basic text of Alcoholics Anonymous is attestation of the value of a spiritual programme of steps and tradition to live by in order to remain sober a day at a time. The Big Book as it is commonly called is a literal bible for alcoholics; those many thousands of men and women whose stories resonate their recovery through following the programme laid down within. The opening chapter of the book tells the stories of the founders; their lives before becoming sober, what happened, and what changed thereafter, bringing hope and recovery from addictive behaviour to themselves and the many who have since its inception in 1935 d this new found freedom for living life on life's terms. For their stories and how this programme evolved I will leave you to read the Big Book at your own discretion.

Suffice to say that Bill Wilson, co-founder, had a spiritual experience of recovery and devoted the majority of his life to helping others suffering Alcoholism to sobriety. The Big Book, written by Bill — aka Bill W. — was first published in 1939, laid the foundation for the 12-step movement that revolutionised addiction treatment and has helped millions of people get and stay sober. With more than 37 million copies sold, the Big Book is one of the bestselling books of all time. Apart from his leadership role as a founder, Bill became a prolific writer of books centred around spirituality, as an advocate of having a God of one's own understanding with guiding literature to supplement his ideas. For Bill's co-founder Doctor Bob Smith, he had but three guiding principles to help alcoholics in their disease. He had them written on the reverse side of his calling card; 1. Trust God. 2 Clean House and 3. Help somebody. Dr Bob saved over 5000 alcoholics back to sobriety who entered the Akron Hospital during his tenure there as resident medical practitioner.

There are many stories in the Big Book of people's lives over the first seventy years of the now worldwide fellowship of AA. They are a worthy read for any suffering soul seeking freedom from bondage. But what of now and what are the promises that are assured to those who follow this spiritual pathway. Well there are twelve of which I shall briefly relate here: 1. We are going to experience a new freedom and new happiness. 2. We will not regret the past nor wish to shut the door on it. 3. We will comprehend the word serenity. 4. We will know peace.5. No matter how far down the scale we have gone, we will see how our experience can benefit others. 6. The feeling of uselessness and self pity will disappear. 7. We will lose interest in selfish things and gain interest in our fellows.8.Self-seeking will slip away. 9. Our whole attitude and outlook on life will change.10. Fear of people and economic insecurity will leave us. 11. We will intuitively know how to handle situations which used to baffle us. And the Pièce de résistance, 12. We will suddenly realise that God is doing for us what we could not do for ourselves.

So let us read now of those who have come from the devastation of being a still practising alcoholic, to finding new hope and peace in their lives. The comments are from both young people in early sobriety and those of longer standing.

"Sobriety has changed my life. It's hard for me to describe it without closing my eyes and getting a little emotional. It has changed every part of my being, the way that I move and the way that I communicate. And the way that I experience things, the way that I cultivate my relationships with people. The way that I decorate myself. It has changed everything for the better. I get to live with both sides of me, the ugly and the good. I can manoeuvre things and figure out what's a good decision for me. The grey area just kind of becomes a little less. There's a whole world that is so celebratory and celebrates you finding your truth. It's a thing where you'll say, "I'm a month sober," and people will be like, *Congratulations!* That's big. Or, like, four days sober. I'm like, *That's so major*. Good for you. There's this whole movement of people. Addiction does not have to be the end of the road — it can actually be a life-changing beginning." (Viewpoint of AA young person in early recovery).

Here is another: " I think it's important to be proud of being sober and to share your story. Just like I talk about anything else going on in my life, this is a part of me. There are a lot of things I love in this world and sobriety is one of them, so I like to talk about that very openly. I don't think it's for everybody and I totally respect that. But for me, I think it's important as a sober person to share this experience and how good it can be. Because a lot of people think we just kind of hide, like you get sober and then you're just detached from the rest of the world. And I don't want people to think that— that's not sobriety to me and is certainly not my experience. I feel more connected with myself and with others than I ever could have imagined. I never really felt like I had a choice in social situations or the people I was around.

I couldn't really sort through who I actually wanted to be around because I felt like I was just along for the ride and I wasn't really in charge. When you're an alcoholic and you're not sober, you feel trapped. It was just one blackout after another, messing up relationships, apologising for things. And it was pretty much that way for 10 years. I look back and am amazed at how long I was OK with settling for that life. Regardless of who you are, what you look like, what you do, your skin colour. It doesn't matter. There is a better way to live." —Sheku

"It's like rolling hills for me. I paint this picture where I got sober and then my life was great. And that's true, partially. I did get sober and my life did get better because it was so low and dark. But that doesn't mean that it's perfect. What it looks like for me is that I now have tools to be a normal, decent human being, which I wasn't before. So sobriety for me is like a bridge back to a normal life. It's not my whole life, but it can be a bridge to where I can reconnect with people in society and I can reconnect with friends and family and use tools that I've learned to engage with another person. Caring less about yourself and caring more about helping others. Having some small impact on someone else's life". -Bill.

"You can either be open about it or be closed off about it and keep it to yourself. And that's what I did when I was drinking: I'd sit in my room home alone. Even when I was out, I'd be in the corner by myself just drinking to isolate or build a wall up. Maybe what I want to do is keep to myself and hide and not talk to anyone about it. But that got me nowhere but the bottom. So then I decided to say, look, there are other people that are still suffering, so why not just talk about it? Maybe I'll yield a different result in the end if I take different actions. So that's why I am so vocal about it. I do it for myself because it helps me feel better and heals me to share and talk about it. But I also do it in case other people don't want to feel alone. Maybe it will remove some stigma if there is someone in the public eye talking about how you can recover from alcoholism and how allies can help their family members recover. You don't have to do it alone. Yeah, it's scary and terrifying and you don't know what to expect so you feel alone in the beginning. That's why it's nice to have people who are visible because then you're like, ``*If they can do it then maybe I can do it too.*" —Kyle

"I was very public about my drinking, so why not be public about the fact that I'm sober and don't drink? I think that's an interesting take on it. In the very beginning I was super loud about it because I needed to be. Like, if I own it then you can't judge me for it. If I own my sobriety then your judgments on it don't matter."

"'I can't tell you how many messages I got in the beginning from people who told me how I've inspired them to maybe not get sober but to live their best life. Or telling me that they've had family members who have died from this or are struggling, and when they see me succeeding with it, it gives them hope that their family member or friend can succeed. Because I didn't see that in my life. And that was really eye opening. Being sober doesn't mean your life is over. Many times when we see posts about sobriety, it's always famous people or before-and-afters of people being a mess and then cleaning up their lives. It's not like, hey, these are real people and they just do it every day. It's not like, hey, I'm normal and I have to do this the exact same way you would if you had to do it." Article extract of sober member.

"My birthday card from my grandma said, "To someone who shows up." First of all, I never would have had a birthday card before. And second of all, it never would have said that. When I had my birthday dinner in New York, someone said that after I got sober, they started to get the best version of me. Every person has qualities that aren't great, but now they get to see me, the best version of me, without all the extra stuff. I feel like I get to be the friend that I want to be. I feel like I show up for people now, and it's huge. I get to be present. I get to ask how you're doing today, and really care about how you're doing today. I want to be an example for everyone. And I just don't want to let people down anymore". —Jordan

"I can share my experience as much as I want, but it's not normal. And I think that's what putting something out in the media does. It puts it into the public eye and passes a value judgement on it and says this is good or this is not good. And most recovery stories are through the lens of rehab, where you might not get to see the beautiful life that you find in sobriety. And the fact of the matter is that now I don't have the option to run away or not pay attention to something that's bothering me. I have to be present and I have to self-reflect and commit to being a better person for the people around me. Alcoholism is a disease that affects relationships, not just the person suffering. It's about you learning how to regrow relationships and care for other people, including yourself." Media article.

"I realise that I don't give myself enough credit. I'm five months sober and I'm also transitioning. I am coming out to family members and really recreating myself to the fullest extent possible. When a person transitions, it's like rebirthing a human. You have to find yourself again. And my relationship with myself has gotten so much deeper, there's so much more to me. The fact that I still believe in life that I'm still here... it's really easy to write off the big things and focus on the small things. And the more that I honour the value that I'm bringing to people's lives, the easier it is for me to stop making bad decisions. It's been very centring and very sobering—that's the best word I can use. Sobriety means clarity. Clear mind, level-headed, not clouded." - as stated by a helping hand.

"Now that I don't have substances to cloud my judgement and I'm seeing myself for who I really am, it's really disheartening sometimes. But it's also very inspiring. Like, look at where I was and look at where I can go. I know I can do so much better. I am made for so much more." —Andrea M.

"I don't think I even really liked drinking — it just seemed to make things a lot easier. And it seemed to make things more fun for a while. Now when people ask, I tell them that it just doesn't suit me... it doesn't do anything for my spiritual state, my mental state, or my creative state. It takes from that and I don't want to play with fire.' Addiction Advertisement.

"I used to really run on adrenaline, which I still do at times, but it's different, and I'm more thoughtful now. I feel more creative and more myself now. It feels like I can create more authentically and show parts of myself that no longer scare me. And that's a big deal to me. I don't want to use my platform to promote sobriety... I want to use my platform to promote being yourself and being authentic and doing what feels right for you, regardless of what's going on around you." —William

"When I first got sober, I spent the first year finally seeing myself in a way that I had been completely unaware of. And I actually felt a huge relief when I realised what my problem was because I felt like I finally had a solution. The pain that I felt in the beginning when I knew I had a problem but didn't know the solution was so, so bad. And actually, it was that pain that caused me to be so willing to do anything for sobriety. I feel like all of the bad decisions that I've made in my life and the things that I did that just did not align with who I am, every one of those was me disconnecting from my soul and walking away from it. So even though the first year sober was the most painful year of my life, I was able to breathe again. Every responsibility I took for my life and every apology I gave helped me to finally feel my soul again. It's like I got to remove those pieces. It's the hardest but most incredible thing I've ever done." —Amy "

Prior to getting sober, I was kind of just lost. I didn't really know what my purpose was. I knew I wanted to do things and I would start to do things, but there was never any follow-through. Because I would start something, get taken over by the disease, and then abandon it. I was always just like, *What am I doing?* I got into the college I wanted to and then dropped out. I got a job I really wanted and then I got fired. I got the relationship I wanted, got the apartment I wanted, I got all of these things that I thought were going to fix me and make me better and I didn't know that I was broken inside, and that's what I needed to heal. So when I got sober, it gave me self-esteem, it gave me worth, it gave me a purpose. I didn't know that I had so much potential to help people. At first it was difficult, but now it's just become my life. My biggest fear was that I was going to get sober and all of my friends and all of my fun would get taken away, because I saw "fun" as going to a bar, blacking out, and waking up somewhere else. And today, I look around and see that I'm actually having fun. So for anyone afraid that they might lose themselves, I can say that I've gotten the opportunity to find myself. That's what I would tell someone: I get to be the best version of myself. I get to take all of that other stuff out of the equation that keeps me from being me. —Armando.

These are but a few personal stories of the healing power of the AA programme. Bringing lost souls back on to a righteous path. It is so easy to fall for the world's values without consideration for the welfare of others. So easy to live in one's own selfish world and perhaps give some chequebook generosity to help the needy, whilst justifying one's existence as proof of life by providing for the family the spoils of financial success. In my case by seeking another drink to fill the unfillable hole in my gut of abandonment and loneliness that only the next drink seems to ease for a time. It took a series of tragic events to cause my fall into a calamity of events I could not find a way out of. The drink was a band aid for a short time to cope, but ultimately I crossed that thin red line into full blown alcoholism, uncontrollable depression and exhausting anxiety.

A self chosen stay in a rehab set me back on the right path again, but it didn't cure me. Ultimately I returned to the drink and once more returned to a recovery ward. This time I cried for help and an answer came in the form of a fellow patient who led me to the doorsteps of AA. It's been 15 years of handing over to a God of my own understanding to guide me, and remaining sober a day at a time through the healing power of Alcoholic Anonymous. I'm happy now, doing what God is guiding me to do in a sober state of mind. It's an evolving process and if one believes in Karma, then it's good karma. And if one believes in grace, then it's the grace of God that rains down upon me if I so choose to believe. I am not saying that it's all grand sailing but I can cope now where in my former life it was a pretence at love, but I was not living it as love for others. It was self(ish) love for what I justified as being necessary for the welfare of those of my family, those I served through my work and the so called fun I was having living a reckless life of a drunkard. Well enough about me of my former life, for I am still on the road to recovery and have a long journey inward yet to manifest into benefit for my fellowman.

The steps of AA are like a miracle in their own right. I believe Bill W's steps to recovery combined with certain prayers as a mantra to live by in accord to a God driven into action lifestyle, are divinely inspired. So irrespective of how one might believe, the recital of prayers attuned to The AA steps are of great benefit to us Alcoholics in our sobriety. The first of these is the Serenity which is said at every meeting of the fellowship: and was written by an American theologian Reinhold Niebuhr (1892-1971). "God, grant me the serenity to accept the things I cannot change, courage to change the things I can, and the wisdom to know the difference. "

It is recognised by alcholics that the first Step is a prayer in itself: "I admit that I am powerless over my addiction and my life is unmanageable when I try to control it. " Jim McLean, now deceased councillor of alcoholics, was not himself an alcoholic, but was a staunch proponent of the benefits of the Big Book in helping addictive patients to recover. Jim once advised me that I would recover if I just lived the 1st step programme. Jim started with much insight: " I (meaning God) can't do it , but Doug can." I took this as a sign that God gave me free will to choose his path to recovery or go on suffering the slings and arrows of outrageous fortune by following my own. It was a matter of recognising that the "I" of me is the link to my Higher Power and Doug in the flesh has the freedom of choice to accept or reject God, anything or everything according to my action or reaction.

So it came to pass that the third step of AA was handed to me at a moment of need in my life by a fellow AA member: "God, I offer myself to Thee - to build with me and do with me as Thou wilt. Relieve me of the bondage of self, that I may better do Thy will. Take away my difficulties, that victory over them may bear witness to those I would help with Thy Power, Thy Love, and Thy Way of Life."

It may do well to remember that the steps of AA are not commandments but merely suggestions on the road to recovery. Step Seven suggests that we "humbly ask God to remove our shortcomings." So the seventh step prayer is very fitting in the matter of being willing to be humble. "My Creator, I am willing that you should have all of me, good and bad. I pray that you now remove from me every single defect of character which stands in the way of my usefulness to you and my fellows. Grant me strength, as I will go out from here, to do your bidding. Amen."

God is all you need.

Let nothing disturb you,

Nothing make you afraid.

All things pass,

God remains.

Be patient,

And you will attain your heart's desire.

With God your own,

You cannot lack

God Suffices.

Amen

From " The Wisdom of St Teresa of Avila", Compiled by Ruth Burrows

CHAPTER 10.

EPILOGUE

This little work started as an aftermath of considering the harm that I had caused in my former life of active alcoholism. It was my willingness to make amends to those persons that led me to my defects of character that resulted in the clearing of bad karma so to speak. It has also helped me to fulfil my wish to erase the bad of all of my life in preference to the good karma that I have come to believe will continue to be forthcoming. This in turn raised the question of suffering and grace that may be bestowed on one once we clear the slate of past wrongdoings and start again. It is not that I necessarily believe in past life karma or indeed the negative and positive effects that such belief in past lives may have on the present one. More to the point it is the facts of my own defects of character and those of my better nature that I speak of in my life over the past seventy plus decades. Karma seems as good a standpoint to start as any other to help me in my pursuit of righteousness, to make amends and to do some self analysis. Using my logical brain I believe I have arrived at the fact that 2 plus 2 equals 'IV.,' in this evaluation. i.e that I have arrived at recognising the good and the bad that lies within me, and how best to understand and put into action the suggested steps of AA for my spiritual betterment and the ultimate benefit of others as an everyday practice. In the teachings of the New Testament it tells of Christ going up to a mountain to pray, to ask God's help in making a big decision. He had to select the chosen twelve from amongst his friends to be his apostles.

The Greek word apóstolos means "one who is sent out," giving it a proper connection with the word apostle, in original English meaning "messengers" referred to as the followers of Jesus. It was twelve of his friends that he chose with the help of God to send out, to carry the message of the gospel to others, that Jesus loved them, that Jesus wants to forgive their defects of character, that Jesus wants to be their friend. So in a kind of way the messenger of the Steps of AA endorse what was advocated by the apostles; the message that God is love, that we can recover from our sufferings and hardships by depending on our Higher power, whoever we may conceive God to be, that we can remain sober a day at a time and help another still suffering alcoholic to sobriety too. In the Apostles' creed, of the Catholic faith it ends with "... I believe in the Holy Spirit the communion of saints, the forgiveness of sins, the resurrection of the body and life everlasting." It could be said another way. I believe in God, in the sacrifice made by Christ in dying on the cross, to give us the grace of the Holy Spirit to rain down upon us for the cleansing of bad karma and the collective communion of good karma. As I believe in the resurrection of the body, one may take this as believing that we the people are the body of Christ here and now, and he will come again to spiritually resurrect us as one body in him into the glory of the heavenly kingdom and life everlasting.

You may call this a wacky way of interpreting my present day association with the scaffolding of my once childhood indoctrination of belief, within the bounds of resurrection being on the same plain as that of past lives, good or bad karma, but it works for me in my logical mind and that is enough for me right now. For I am more attuned to the creative mind of the manifestation of a risen Christ than the reality or not of the biblical one.

It is taking me a long time to listen with my mind and body attuned to the rhythm of life, of nature and the miracle of the earth in which we live. This listening comes in the form of meditation, prayer, and yoga practice, or indeed from the mind of fellow AAs who give of themselves in helping me understand what it is that I need to know and do for my spiritual well being and for others in whom we serve in the fellowship of AA. For me my fellow AAs are 'Apostles,' be they believers in God, the power within the bounds of AA, or the natural ways of the earth, space and the universe at large.

I am still on a learning curve, ever mindful of the dangers of letting my will run riot over all I am advocating here. For my own spiritual betterment is ever dependent upon the fellowship of AA, the message it distributes through its members, my friends on a righteous path. I do not have to agree with the viewpoints of my fellows as they relate to the world at large. Indeed I do not have to like them, nor is it necessary for them to like me. What is important is that we are all on the same wavelength when it comes to putting into practice the suggested steps of AA, its traditions and the values we inherit by knowing one another. Friendship more often than not prevails, but I am right now to let go and let God as taught in AA, as to deficiencies in my fellow man. Forgiving them more now than when I professed traditional beliefs in my drinking days.

I trust that you the reader get some benefits for your own spiritual wellbeing in the reading of this book.

About the Author.

Doug McPhillips, poet, singer, songwriter, author, commenced his journey of discovery over a decade ago after many adventures across Spain, Ireland, Pacifica, New Zealand and Australia.

Doug has recorded his many songs inspired by his journeys interrelated with majestic melody in true Australian style. He has written six books, and an autobiography apart from this latest novel.

Doug divides his time in his latter years to continuing to review tasks in maintaining the benefits of adventure on his website caminoway.com.au and in building opportunities for emerging artist musicians to help promote their work. His latest adventure is called 'one to be in studio' under the brand logo 12BN STUDIO.COM

This book is printed by IngramSpark La Verge Tennessee, USA and can be purchased on demand internationally as a paperback at any bookstore or read online as an ebook through the caminoway.com.au book page and the website 12BNStudio.com as an audio. It is available through online book stores and retailers .

D.McP May 23.

www.ingramcontent.com/pod-product-compliance
Lightning Source LLC
Chambersburg PA
CBHW061138010526
44107CB00069B/2980